Unlocking the Growth

You will be amazed at your church's potential

Michael Harvey
with Rebecca Paveley

MONARCH
B O O K S

Oxford, UK & Grand Rapids, Michigan, USA

Published by Monarch Books (an imprint of Lion Hudson plc)
Wilkinson House, Jordan Hill Road, Oxford OX2 8DR, England
email monarch@lionhudson.com; www.lionhudson.com/monarch
and by Elevation (an imprint of the Memralife Group)
Memralife Group, 14 Horsted Square, Uckfield, East Sussex TN22 1QG
Tel: +44 (0)1825 746530; Fax +44 (0)1825 748899; www.elevationmusic.com

ISBN 978 0 85721 198 9 (print)
ISBN 978 0 85721 279 5 (epub)
ISBN 978 0 85721 278 8 (Kindle)

Acknowledgments
Unless otherwise stated, Scripture quotations taken from the *Holy Bible, New
International Version*, copyright © 1973, 1978, 1984 by the International Bible Society.
Used by permission of Zondervan and Hodder & Stoughton Limited. All rights
reserved. The 'NIV' and 'New International Version' trademarks are registered in
the United States Patent and Trademark Office by International Bible Society. Use of
either trademark requires the permission of International Bible Society. UK trademark
number 1448790. Scripture quotations marked KJV are taken from The Authorized
(King James) Version. Rights in the Authorized Version are vested in the Crown.
Reproduced by permission of the Crown's patentee, Cambridge University Press.

A catalogue record for this book is available from the British Library.

Printed and bound in the UK, May 2013, LH26

Michael Harvey is an internationally recognized mission expert, speaker and coach. Michael has trained thousands of church leaders, both clergy and lay, and played a part in mobilizing 500,000 accepted invitations to church. It is estimated that over 50,000 people have been added to the church on eight individual days. In 2004, he assumed the role of developer of Back to Church Sunday across England, working in the Back to Church Sunday National Team. From 2007, he began Back to Church Sunday in Australia, New Zealand, Canada, France, Holland, Ireland, Wales, and Scotland. He is planning missions in Africa and amongst the native American Indians in the near future. He is itinerant and receives no salary.

Rebecca Paveley is a journalist who has written for the *Daily Mail*, *The Times* and the *Church Times*. She has also worked as a press adviser to the former Bishop of Oxford, the Rt Revd Richard Harries, and currently advises the Bishop of Exeter, the Rt Revd Michael Langrish.

Unlocking the Growth Trust
The Trust has been founded to educate the Christian church in seeking to encourage the mobilization of every church member to invite. See www.unlockingthegrowth.com

For the millions of people who need
a simple invitation.
And to my family Eike, Ben, Kirsty
and Lydia without whom none
of what follows would have been
possible.

Contents

Foreword

This book is about helping churches re-learn how to make disciples. A challenge from the "Back to Church Sunday" initiative, it goes right to the heart of what it is to be church, namely, worshipping God and infecting his world with the goodness of Jesus Christ. Ever since Philip first urged Nathanael to "come and see" (John 1:46) the practice of invitation has been crucial to spreading of the Gospel of Jesus Christ.

When I was Bishop for Stepney in the East End of London, one of the Hackney churches sported a sign that had been erected years before carrying this stark message for the parishioners: "This is your church." Since that sign went up, just after the Second World War, the urban parish around it has changed many times over. Initially there was the struggle of clearing up after wartime bombing, the years of rationing, then the beginnings of greater prosperity. Along with this went the gradual exodus of many of the original inhabitants, the arrival of new communities, initially from the Carribbean and soon from every continent. Then followed a succession of urban renewal schemes with greater or lesser degrees of success. The "you" to which the sign was addressed was constantly changing, but what did the church mean by addressing its parishioners in this way? Crucially, what sort of invitation was on offer?

At worst, I am afraid, at times it meant: "This is your church because you live here, come and help us pay our way!"

Or at best, it meant: "This church is all yours – come here if you will, and make yourself at home." Happily there are some of those who first arrived from the Caribbean still worshipping there, for whom that church stood out then as a place of welcome in an otherwise hostile community. A place of hospitality, refuge, and hope.

Or was it in fact an invitation, though written for those outside to read, which had to be read from the inside too? After all, congregations can all too easily settle for claiming the church for their own, a refuge from the big bad world outside. The Church, as Archbishop William Temple said, is a community unique in this, in that "it exists for the benefit of those who are not yet its members." It is as if we are saying to everyone, this is your church – it is not just for us, in fact we are incomplete without you. God is giving you an invitation to come and be guests of Christ, whose Church it is. Running the risk of cliché, it is as that other "hackneyed" wayside pulpit asks, Ch...ch? Who is missing? – UR.

This book will help churches reconsider their relationship with the people they serve, and for whom they bear witness to the love of God in Christ. It offers the building blocks for a culture change, practical steps towards becoming an inviting, engaging, hospitable church where people make friends with each other and with God.

The challenge, at the end of the day, is still the question, whose church is it? Learning to attract, engage, and nurture new worshippers is a vital step towards an even greater goal, the transformation of whole communities with the love of God in Christ – the Kingdom of God, something much bigger than what we call church. I pray that all who read this book will see their church fellowships growing both in numbers and in spiritual maturity to make a difference, and that they will be inspired to join in.

+Sentamu Ebor

Acknowledgments

Bringing a book to life requires teamwork. The author would like to thank Rebecca Paveley, who has spent long hours improving the manuscript and encouraging me to expand my thinking.

Thank you also to the team at Monarch: Tony Collins, who persisted with a first time author, and Jenny Ward.

The Back to Church Sunday Team: Gillian Oliver, Bishop Paul Bayes, Nigel Spraggins, Nicola James, Revd Nick Devenish, Karen Smith, and Jane Riley, who have worked so hard in getting simple invitation onto the agenda.

In Australia thanks go to Bishop Stuart Robinson, who was the first to pilot invitation, and to Bishop Andrew Curnow and Bishop Stephen Hale, who invited me to a Bishops Conference.

In Canada thanks go to Revd John Lockyer for the first pilot and to Bishop Philip Poole, who saw the potential.

In New Zealand to Revd Tony Gerritsen, with whom I spent one of the best weeks of my life taking invitation across the two islands, and to Claire Onslow, who can recite my seminar from memory.

I have met so many brilliant men and women of God in my journeys and I wish I could mention all of you.

But above all thanks to the hundreds of thousands of Christians who have attempted an invitation for the sake of the extension of God's kingdom.

Preface

This book is about how to unleash growth in our churches by doing something so simple that a child could – and often does – do.

It's about simply inviting a friend with you to church. Maybe you do this on a regular basis anyway. If you do, then you could stop reading this right now.

But if you are one of the millions of churchgoers who find it difficult to do this, then I hope this book may give you the confidence to try. At the time of writing, I have been involved with an initiative called Back to Church Sunday for eight years. The initiative has seen an estimated 250,000 people accept invitations to church. For some of these people the invitation will have been the end of a long journey; for others it may have been the first time they have attended an ordinary service of worship. Some of those invited may stay, some may not come back. If nothing else, I hope this book will help us to judge success not by the numbers who stay, but by the number of people we actually ask.

I don't believe in church growth. Now, that might sound odd, given that this book has the aim of growing the church! What I do believe is that God gives the growth, but we sometimes "lock it down".

What does this mean? Here's an example. Around 250 years ago a young man challenged the church authorities of the day, because he wanted to take the good news out to the nation and he didn't mind preaching in the open air or stepping across parish boundaries. The church leadership of the time tried to stop him, and encouraged other church leaders to whip up opposition. Nowadays, we look back with great fondness on John Wesley and believe God raised him up for the work. But the church leaders of the day wanted to lock down God's work through Wesley. They just didn't know that they had *the* John Wesley in their midst![1]

This locking down is often to do with us, frankly, being unaware of how blinkered we are. We don't know what we don't know, and it takes a moment of epiphany to show us what has been obvious to others all along. Sometimes we lock down through fear, but we may not be aware of this until it is brought to the surface. Later, I will explore the idea that there could be ungodly thoughts, or rubbish, which reveal the lock that is preventing us from moving on. As Jesus points out, in the verse about the speck and log in Matthew 7:1–5, it is easy to see other people's rubbish but much more difficult to see our own.

But it is worth making the effort. I have seen how removing this rubbish can lead to churches doubling or even trebling their congregations in a day. The lock was a limiting vision: replace it with a high-expectation vision, and the growth is unstoppable. People have overcome their fear of rejection by facing this fear head on and asking friends and relatives to church. I have also seen the expectations of people invited to church surpassed by what they describe afterwards as a wonderful experience. Locks exist at every level, from the first thoughts about inviting someone, through to the acceptance of that invitation.

Often the most dramatic results occur when people are made aware of what they are thinking, believing, and expecting, and they can then see how this affects their actions. I think these locks are actually what some of the Church Fathers called sins of omission. In our generation, the church is fixated with sins of commission, the supposed big sins which everyone can see, but the sins of omission are equally debilitating. And as they can be hidden away, they don't get brought to repentance.

The whole process of unlocking growth reveals the things we ought to do but we don't do. We need a specific confession of where we miss the mark in our inner life. We need to recognize the sins of omission – what we don't do but ought to – confess them to God, repent, and then move in the opposite direction. If we don't do this, the sin or limiting practice appears in a different guise at a later stage. If we think it is important to keep short accounts with God, then we need to pay attention to what we are thinking and how that is affecting our life of service with God.

There are parallels with the story of the children of Israel leaving Egypt. They left behind their homes and a lifestyle that was secure in its own way, at least compared with being in the desert. And the further they went on the journey the more attractive their old life seemed, even as slaves! At many points on the journey, they wanted to go back to Egypt. We can all get so comfortable with our lifestyles, our bank accounts, our homes, and our careers, that we don't want to change, despite the fact that we are living lives way below our God-given potential. Even if we know our lives aren't that great, we are comfortable with them, and for many of us it is very difficult to unlock the potential within.

There is a science called Neuroplasticity which looks at how our brain works. It studies how the human brain changes as a result of experience. Scientists have discovered the brain is "plastic" and "malleable", when they'd previously thought it did not change after the critical period of childhood. They've discovered, in effect, that our brain is not hard-wired.[2]

Now, frankly, any student of the Bible could have told scientists that! After all, we have Bible verses such as "be transformed by the renewing of your mind" (Romans 12:2). Scientists have done work with stroke victims and there is growing evidence that the brain can be trained to compensate for dead or damaged areas. They've discovered that each time stroke victims repeat a movement or action, a pathway in the brain is formed initially just as a scratch, but it becomes deeper and deeper until it becomes automatic, a habit.

We can use this discovery to focus our attention on what we want to change, and then repeat it frequently enough to make new connections and pathways.

However, just as the journey from Egypt to the Promised Land was fraught with difficulties, our individual journeys to unlocking our God-given potential and finding freedom in Christ will have obstacles in the way. In fact, very often we will yearn to go back to the comfort and safety of our former lives. Are you willing to step out of your comfort zone with me, and try?

Chapter 1

Will You Come Along?

Stuart still lived at home with his parents. He spent his days working, going to the pub, eating his mum's home-cooked food and watching TV. He'd never given a thought to God. But one day, a girl at work came up to him and invited him to church. He surprised himself by saying yes – perhaps he thought he was being asked on a date! Elsie picked him up on Sunday morning and took him with her to church. When she asked him afterwards what he thought of the service, he just described it as "OK". He met some of Elsie's friends and was invited to their homes for meals over the next few weeks.

He came back again, and then again, and then was given a Bible by Elsie, who was leaving to go home to South Africa. Stuart started to ask questions that he said later he never knew he had inside him.

Stuart went on to become an active member of that church. Years later he said that Elsie's invitation and the hospitality of her friends made a dramatic difference in his life, and today Stuart can still be found at the very same church to which he was invited years ago.

A recent survey by the charity Tearfund found that in

the UK alone there are 3 million people like Stuart (and many more in the USA, Canada, Australia and New Zealand) who would go to church if only they were asked to do so by a friend. Do you know any of them? You may think you don't but it is very likely you do. It might be a work colleague, a fellow parent at your child's school, or your next-door neighbour but one, who is just waiting for you to pluck up the courage to ask them.

In the years I have been going round churches speaking on the themes of invitation and welcome, I have heard hundreds of personal stories that have convinced me that God is preparing people every day for an invitation. I have heard from people who go past church buildings every day of their lives, who are curious about what happens inside, or for whom the building brings back childhood memories of church, but they don't dare come in. It takes a very brave person to walk into a church on their own, yet we can be sure that God is speaking to them, and perhaps all they need is a gentle invitation from someone they know.

I have often wondered exactly when it became difficult for people outside church to cross the threshold of their local church building. Once the church was the centre of the community. Nowadays we hear people say that they would feel hypocritical if they came. This self-disqualification is reinforced by their non-churchgoing friends. This feeling of being hypocritical can be overcome through simple invitation. I have even recommended holding a service of prayer and blessing over the threshold of a church building, to pray into the fear on both sides of the threshold.

An "Invitation Sunday" is really a very odd mission! It's a mission to those in the church already, not those who are outside it. We aim to reach the people who aren't in church through those who already are.

But the beauty of it is that it is so simple. You don't have to go on a training course, or agree to wear a special uniform. The thought of unleashing the potential God has placed in each one of us through this simplest of activities is incredible. In Luke 10:1–16, when Jesus sent seventy-two disciples out on a mission, He trusted each one of them to be all that God had intended them to be. When they returned, they shared their surprise and amazement at what they'd experienced. These ordinary men saw and felt the power of the kingdom of God. But the more wonderful thing about this story is the fact that Jesus sent them. He wanted them to share in this simple form of mission. He showed us that mission is not God doing things on His own. He has of course prepared the way, but we also have a part to play. So in the same way that Jesus asked the seventy-two to go ahead of Him, today God is asking us to play our part in His work in our generation. And our part, often, is just to invite.

The success of an Invitation Sunday lies in one person inviting one person. And remarkably, it does *not* rely on one person inviting one person and that person saying "yes". The answer to the invitation is in God's hands. One of my favourite authors, Jim Rohn, says: "God has the tough end of the deal. What if instead of planting the seed you had to make the tree? That would keep you up late at night, trying to figure that one out."[1]

We should not take responsibility for the answer – and yet so often we do, or we try to. We worry about whether they will accept or not, and read into their answer all sorts of criticisms of ourselves. But the reality is, some people will say yes and some people will say no… and we have to get over any disappointment we might feel.

We prove success by measurable results. Now this sounds a bit too harsh and exact for a church, perhaps. But remember that somebody actually counted how many people were added to the church on the day of Pentecost (Acts 2:41), and that somebody counted the number of fish caught after Jesus had asked the disciples to fish on the other side (see John 21 for the full story). Measuring what happens helps us to hear God's voice. God is speaking to us when something doesn't go so well, and so to count or measure our results can be helpful in hearing from Him the next steps we are to take. By not measuring, reflecting and re-envisioning, we can often move on too quickly and may miss the move God wants us to make.

I first became involved with the idea of an Invitation Sunday when I picked up a phone call from my friend Gillian Oliver, then the Communications Director for the Bishop of Manchester, who had been searching for ways to get the church moving forward. I was immediately taken with the idea, not just because of the simplicity of it but because of the excitement I heard in Gillian's voice.

When the name "Back to Church Sunday" first came up, we thought that what God might be calling us to do was to provide a bridge to those who had drifted away from the church. The name "Back to Church" gives this impression. And over the years the main focus of the initiative has been on this group of people, who are returning to church, some after months, some after years, but many after decades. Yet in the second year of the initiative, in 2005, we started to hear from people who had never been to church before, but who had been invited to come on this Sunday anyway, and had stayed. Originally the focus of the initiative had been those who were lapsed churchgoers, but now God showed us how He wants to use our idea by inviting those He has been working with outside church. So why do we continue to call it Back to Church Sunday? Some people have asked for a name change and have suggested that if only it was changed to "Come to Church Sunday", then thousands would turn up on the doorsteps of our churches!

But I still don't think it was a mistake calling it Back to Church Sunday. The "Back" refers to the momentum coming from God the Father to our generation. You see, God wants us all "back" into a relationship with Him. This is all about Him. Now in every generation there is a momentum coming from Him. We can look back three or four generations and say the pressure to attend church came from society in the days when most people went to church (because it was what people did in those days). Move on a couple of generations and the momentum changed; many people sent their children to church, but they didn't go themselves any longer. But there was still a momentum. Now we look at our generation and see that neither adults nor their children are coming to our acts of worship in great numbers any longer. But despite that, our God is still at work. In fact He is speaking to more people *outside* the four walls of our church buildings than He is *inside*. In our generation we need to connect with God's momentum through personal invitation. So the "Back" in Back to Church Sunday is not all about us, or those we invite, but about Him.

The "Church" in Back to Church Sunday is not the building, and is not even the act of worship. Church is the gathered people of God in a community, helping to nurture a relationship with God the Father. Now I love participating in worship but it is part of church, not the whole of church. Yet in many places throughout the world we have made the act of worship the only expression of church.

The "Sunday" of Back to Church Sunday is there because I think we have a curse hanging over the church today. It is a word we should not use lightly, so let me explain. The curse that I believe is hanging over the Western church is the mindset which talks about those outside church and says: "If they wanted to come, they would come." The focused Invitation Sunday helps us to overcome the curse, by focusing on being invitational on one day *together*. It may seem a bit forced at first, but after doing it once it will become more natural. We need the focus at first of one Sunday in the year to get us out of the habit of not inviting. At the moment, unfortunately, many of our congregations simply hope that the someone will come into their church and take over the running of it, saving them the bother. They are sitting back and waiting for people to come through the doors, quoting this curse that if they really wanted to, people would come. It continually reminds them that people used to come in the past and didn't need an invitation.

Now why is this a curse? If we look back to what God our Father did in past generations, when our forefathers built large church buildings to accommodate the communities they served, the very construction of a church building attracted people to come. When the buildings were first put up they would have been packed. Now the fact that people aren't coming in such great numbers leads us to conclude that they don't want to come. But we must remember what a difficult step it is for many just to walk through the door without having been invited in. It takes a very brave (or perhaps desperate) person to come into a church building on their own nowadays, but this doesn't mean that God is not at work in the lives of these people. He is just asking us to connect with the work He is already doing.

Christ is alive and active among our friends, family and community. We need to go and invite them, and accept that some people will leap at our invitation and some won't.

Jim Currin of Churches Together in England and Wales wrote:

> *BBC and Open University conducted a survey in the*
> *UK which invited people to say what Christianity*

means to them. The results are very revealing.

The introduction to the survey reminds us that 71.6% of the UK population described themselves as Christian in the 2001 Census, although only 15% of that number belong to, or go to church. Interestingly, the questionnaire is designed to ask people who call themselves Christian why they do not attend.

The questions make it difficult to fill in if you do go to church. The results probably produce a bias which is less representative of the church-going population as a whole, which presumably makes the various conclusions all the more encouraging to people like me.

At the time of checking the survey results in 2009, of those who had taken part up to that point, 75% said they call themselves Christians to other people, and a further 18% would sometimes say so to their friends. These figures are very high which is not surprising as prompted by a programme about the Christian faith.

More striking though, if I have read the results right, is that nearly twice as many men as women have completed the questionnaire: 2114 compared to 1125. I am not sure what that says: do more men watch the programme or take part in online surveys? Virtually all are from the UK as only 207 say they are not.

In passing, I was also interested to see the distribution across the age groups. Apart from the under 20s where 216 questionnaires were completed, and the over 70s where 126 replied online, the twenties

(533), thirties (575), forties (644), fifties (637) and sixties (508) provide a fairly even spread.

The first thing to note is that more than half of the respondents go to church every week and pray every day. No doubt they are the most motivated to complete the questionnaire but remember they have been discouraged in the introduction. More than ¾ pray more than once a month. Of the survey target audience nearly half do not attend church regularly, so what have they to say to us all?

When asked why the people don't go to church, the least significant reason is lack of time and peer pressure, while many more say that they "don't feel comfortable" or [have] "not found [a] church that suits me", or simply "don't need to go to church to be a Christian".

Having said that, significantly for such initiatives as "Back to Church Sunday" or any "Invitation Sunday", 57% of respondents then said they would go more often if they could. Chiefly, for these people, what stops them is work, family and other commitments, rather than the church itself.

I find all this very encouraging when the invitation is for people who don't go to church to respond and more men than women have done so, and more than half would go more often if they could.[2]

There is a huge constituency of people who don't attend church now who were once part of a church. Some postmodern

Christian thinkers suggest this is the last generation, or we are now past the last generation, of people who know much about church or the stories from the Bible, but there is still a surprising resilience among the general population who, in survey after survey, census after census, decide to call themselves Christian. I have a theory about this.

I think the blessings of the church over past generations are affecting us today. A passage in the Old Testament says the sins of the fathers go to the third and fourth generation (Exodus 20:5). If that is true, then could it be true of blessings also? One of the most powerful blessings is that said during the baptism service: "I sign you with the sign of the cross. Christ claims you for His own." This is one of many blessings which have been said over countless adults and children throughout countless generations. Even if our generation has never had this blessing said directly over them, perhaps it doesn't matter. Even if their parents, or grandparents, have never had it said over them, it doesn't matter. Somewhere along the line, back through generations of our families, somebody has had a powerful blessing said over them. And that blessing may still have power today. It links people to the Christian church in some way still. And it might suggest why, in every census in the Western world, when people can freely choose the box that says "No religion", they still choose to tick the box that declares them to be Christian. Many – if not most – of these people have rarely darkened the doorstep of the church, but they still identify themselves as Christian. Who moves the hand that moves the pen to tick the box?

The resilience of these people who don't go to church but still identify themselves as Christian is quite remarkable. It suggests to me that someone is holding them fast. We should take inspiration from this to become an inviting person in an invitational church, and to believe that God has prepared His people for invitation. When Jesus said "Follow me" to those first disciples as He started His ministry, He was revealing to us the invitational nature of His Father.

Interestingly, this huge constituency of people who are open to an invitation to attend church are not just the families and the young people the church can often target its mission at, but also includes the retired and the soon to be retired. Thousands of people every day in the UK are turning sixty. In the days immediately before and after their birthday, they are probably going through a process that sounds something like this:

- Stage 1: "How on earth did I get to be sixty?"
- Stage 2: "Whew, I've got a couple more decades!"
- Stage 3: "Wow! That's all happened fast. Will the next twenty years go so fast, and when will I do something that matters?"

Just as God uses the birth of a child or a wedding to remind people of His constant presence in our lives, He also uses key dates, including some of the big birthdays! By holding invitational Sundays, activities or events, we are working in an area where God has already been working and we are reaping the benefits of His work.

Questions to think about

- Who moves the hand that moves the pen to tick the box "Christian" on the census form?

- Are people open to an invitation to come along?

- Do you agree with Michael that there is a "curse" hanging over the church which says, "If they wanted to come to our act of worship they would come"?

- What is the outcome of this "curse"?

Chapter 2

The Reasons Why We Don't Invite Our Friends

Remember when you first brought your girlfriend or your boyfriend back to meet your parents? Do you remember worrying, "Will my parents like him/her? Will they get on? Or will they embarrass me in front of my girlfriend/boyfriend?"

When you introduce your friend to church, you go through the same sort of worry. You fear that if it doesn't go well, your friend may not like you any more. This kind of introduction takes the friendship to a different level and we are anxious. What will our friend say when they meet our church friends? What will they think about the service? Will it be too long? Will something go wrong? Will someone get up and say something that just makes you cringe?

Donald Rumsfeld, the former US Secretary of Defense, got up one morning, and while probably still in his slippers and dressing-gown, went to a microphone and spoke to the world, saying:

> *There are known knowns. These are things we know*
> *that we know. There are known unknowns. That is to*
> *say, there are things that we know we don't know. But*
> *there are also unknown unknowns. There are things we*
> *don't know we don't know.*[1]

Take a moment to think about that quote! Some of us get to an age in life where, frankly, we're sure we know it all. We've lived a lot and we've learnt that if we carry out a certain action, we can predict what the result is going to be. We've become very experienced. When we were young, naïve and inexperienced we used to try things for God. But now we know better: we've become experienced. We're too learned to try something out for the first time – and we are especially cautious if it seems to be so simple. We distrust what seems simple and look for the failure that we expect to be lurking in the background.

So do we think we know it all or can we believe that we are all to some degree unconsciously incompetent? Have we as a church congregation stopped learning? We have had a problem at an institutional level for decades with inviting people to church, yet we have never spent time reviewing why we have this problem. A lack of reflective learning is one of the major "locks" on the church today. We move on too quickly and we forget that God speaks through failure. We all have unknown unknowns, yet sometimes we act as if we haven't, and so we don't ever look at issues that are holding us back, such as our failure to invite.

The locks

So why don't people invite their friends to church? Here are a few reasons which I call the "congregational locks" – the issues that are holding us back, as members of the congregation, from inviting our friends and neighbours to church.

At the hundreds of seminars I have conducted I have used two keys to reveal congregational locks and then deal with them. Key one is discovery, asking: Why do you think your congregation are not inviting their friends? This results in the following extensive list. The second key is asking for forgiveness, because when you examine the list carefully you will find a sin of omission. Do you recognize any of these objections from yourself or your congregation?

1. "I suffer and I don't want my friend to suffer" and "My friend won't want to go"

We can all remember being present at excruciating or embarrassing services. Some of us have even led them! When we think about inviting our friends to church, we remember those services and then imagine inviting our friends to something like that. Maybe we worry what our friend will think of us when they know we are involved in a church like that. We conclude it would be better not to put our friendship on the line, and not to invite them after all.

But when we consider this lock in more detail we will find that while it might have a semblance of truth about it, it is not the whole truth.

Firstly, we are making the decision whether to invite our friends on the basis of how we feel about our own act of worship. We are so Christian about issuing an invitation that we save our friends the bother of saying "no" to a question we are not going to ask them!

Secondly, our friend is unlikely to see the same issues or problems that we are likely to see.

Thirdly, it says something about our own experience of church that God might be wanting to address. But because of this paralysing attitude we do not invite our friend.

2. "I don't want to be rejected"

Many of us at some point in our lives have actually plucked up the courage to invite a friend to church with us, but they've turned down our invitation. No one wants to hear the word "no". It is a rejection. All our lives, we do what we can to avoid rejection; we steer away from exposing the innermost workings of our hearts. At this point in my seminars I usually ask the audience whom they know who was rejected. And not just rejected, but scorned, beaten and shamed. Jesus suffered all these things. And if we are following the path of faith, at times we will be rejected – period. As followers of Christ we need to discipline our disappointment and to press on for Him.

I have been rejected hundreds if not thousands of times. When a rejection occurs, I start taking it personally, and after a number of rejections – when I should be used to it – I can tend to mope a bit. But I have a phrase to help me to move on.

I say to myself, "Isn't that interesting?" It sounds a bit silly, but saying it helps me to distance myself from the rejection and move on.

Do we live by fear and not by faith, because we fear being rejected? FEAR stands for false (F) evidence (E) appearing (A) real (R). Fear is a thief that steals and destroys but it will only become big if we allow it to grow. We can stop it growing by recognizing it, then we can resist it, then we can reject it.

I have also learnt that NO means (N)ext (O)ne!

3. "We have no non-church-going friends"

This is often the first line of defence and while there will of course be some truth in it, it will not be wholly true. We overcome this reservation through Step 6 of the twelve steps described in Chapter 4. (Step 6 encourages us to ask God to prompt us or give us an impression of the person He has prepared in advance for us to invite.) Within each one of us is a reservoir of potential. Only we have the unique relationships to reach our friendship group, and we need to recognize a debilitating thought when we hear ourselves saying it, and challenge it.

4. "It's the church leader's job!"

"In fact, what on earth are we paying them for if they are not into mission?" I have heard of church management meetings where fingers are pointed very firmly in the direction of the church leader. We must remember, however, that when we start pointing the finger, three fingers are pointed straight back at us. Jesus invited the seventy-two into mission. He invites all of us into mission. Now mission is a large concept about which many books have been written. At the centre of most expressions of mission is invitation, and invitation is something we can all do. It is most definitely not just the church leader's job.

5. "My friend said no to me last year"

Why do we give up so easily? I have heard countless stories from Christians who had to be asked several times before they accepted an invitation. We need to learn from the persistence shown in the story of the lost coin or the lost sheep. There was a true persistence and a determination shown in these stories. But remember too that success is the invitation, not the answer.

6. "I was never invited – I was born into the church"

We have all been invited, we just don't realize it at times. I was invited by my mother, repeatedly – sometimes when I least wanted to hear it! We need to remember who invited us and the blessing that has been in our lives, so that we might pass the blessing along in our turn.

7. "What if it damages my friendship?"

A fear of spoiling a good relationship is another lock. We don't ask because we fear the damage it might cause – perhaps irreparable damage. We worry what our friend might think of us, after he or she has experienced a service. It is very unlikely that we are going to spoil a true relationship over a simple invitation. Of course, it might change the relationship for the better.

8. "Our services and people are unpredictable"

We want to know in advance who is preaching, whether the right hymns will be sung, and whether everyone will behave. We are not going to invite someone unless everything is perfect that day! We anticipate in advance the worst thing that could happen and assume it will, so we don't invite because of this assumption. Church, of course, is more than the act of worship, so we can introduce our friends to friends in the congregation.

9. "I fear the congregation will think my friend is not 'our' type of person"

"What if it damages my relationship with my friends in church when they see the type of person I am friendly with outside?" We shouldn't forget that Jesus spent time with tax collectors and those who were the outcasts of society, to the amazement and horror of the religious leaders of the day.

10. "No empty seats near me"

"Where would my friend sit? It's already fairly packed on some Sundays." This is just an excuse not to invite, and it's possibly the weakest argument of all. After all, what happened to folding chairs?

11. "It will be boring"

We think, "I just can't imagine how my friend would not find what we do on a Sunday morning boring. I do!" This is a classic example of making decisions on behalf of our friends and doing the thinking for them, to stop us from having to invite them.

12. "I'm shy"

"I am a fairly shy person and, frankly, I would find it difficult to invite somebody else." How did Jesus' command to "go and make disciples" fit in with a shy and reticent personality? For most of us, whether we are shy or not, inviting someone does cause us to worry. However, whether we are worried, shy or fearful, doing the things that make us afraid can make the fear go away.

13. "Faith is a private thing"

We were all taught as youngsters that there are three things that we do not mention in polite society: sex, politics and religion. Our faith is seen as a private thing and we assume everybody else has been taught the same. But where in the Bible and church history does it say that our faith is to be private?

14. "I don't want to be seen as strange"

"I don't want to be seen as a Bible-basher, or worse, one of those fundamentalists." Each of us wants to be thought of as a sane person. At times in the Christian life we will be rejected and seen as odd. We have to get over this; we have to be willing to stand up and be counted.

15. "I wouldn't know what to say"

"How do you go about asking someone to church, and what if they ask me a question that I am unable to answer, like 'Explain the Trinity'?!" We start to imagine all the difficult questions that might be asked after we've stumbled through an invitation, and we decide that it is not worth the effort, after all. Often we feel we need a lot of training on what we say to our friends, and this becomes a convenient reason not to invite them. The training in Step 7 of the twelve steps will take ten seconds.

16. "They need to be the right people"

"Frankly, my friends are not the right type of people for our church. They would have to believe first, and even then their behaviour would just be unacceptable to the rest of the congregation." You do wonder at times whether somebody who turns over tables in the temple is the "right person" for our church!

17. "Inviting is a brilliant idea"

This is a subtle lock, where you think you have convinced congregational members to invite. But in the end they don't. This is called the blancmange effect. When you hit blancmange it wobbles back to the same position. It is immune to moving position! Some congregational members can appear really enthusiastic about the idea, but they are still not going to do it, and it will be as if you have never mentioned it. Beware blancmange Christianity!

18. "They might ask me about my faith and why I go to church!"

Many of us are afraid not so much about getting a "no", but about getting an actual response to the question. Now this is a wonderful lock – it's not truly a problem at all. Being asked why we go to church will help us to express the faith within us. Some of us have a faith like the apostle Andrew's. He had spent only a short time with Jesus – just a few hours – yet there was something about those few hours that ignited something in him. For some of us, our faith will be like that of Thomas, with plenty of doubts and uncertainties among the deep certainties. Others of us will find ourselves capable of bold declaration, like Peter, who was able to declare that Jesus was indeed the Son of God. For others of us the question will cause us to really ask why in fact we do go to church. We should not be afraid of this question – rather, we should relish it. But perhaps we need to start thinking about the answer!

Locks that church leaders face

So we've looked at some of the locks that stop church congregations inviting. But there are locks stopping us inviting at every level. Let's look at some that come from church leaders. Here I've used some actual quotes that I've been given.

1. "We're dreadful at inviting people"

This was given as a reason why this church leader was never, ever, going to do an Invitation Sunday again! The question is, are we into failure or feedback? This is the crunch time, the true test of leadership. It is during a crisis that the leader emerges. You can look at that statement in two ways. With a failure mindset, you would agree with the sentiment. With a feedback mindset, you look for the opportunity. Well, this could be the training opportunity for which this church leader has been waiting. Let's look at why we are "dreadful"; let's see whether it is true that we are "dreadful". Perhaps we could ask another church leader how their church overcame their dread of invitation.

When things go wrong – and they will in leadership – it is actually a wonderful gift from God. It's a real opportunity to learn. When things go wrong, it is like God sending us our own training programme. It is opportunity knocking on our door. Opportunity to learn does not knock once but all the time. So here are seven things to do in crunch time:

1. Stay calm.

2. Get the facts. (Ask questions until you have all the information.)

3. Take responsibility. (I am responsible.)

4. Remain confident. (God never sends us a problem that is too big for us.)

5. Unleash creativity. (How can we solve this problem?)

6. Concentrate on priorities. (What is the one thing we need to do?)

7. Counter-attack. (Take action.)

One of the greatest discoveries that any church leader can make is that church members can alter their lives by altering their thoughts. Proverbs 23:7 says, "For as he thinketh in his heart, so is he" (KJV). Philippians 4:8 encourages us to fill our minds with good things. Isaiah 55:7 says, "Let the wicked forsake his way and the evil man his thoughts." We need to take responsibility for our own thinking. Now some of our thinking will be difficult to overcome, but we should remain confident because, as Psalm 27:1 says, God is the strength of our life. This is how we start to unleash the creativity of ourselves as leaders and our congregations to start to solve the problem of poor thinking. We need to concentrate on reducing the amount of error within our thought life and replace it with a flow of new thoughts. As God reveals the poor thinking, we need to concentrate on replacing it by asking for forgiveness and then repent and turn in a new direction.

2. "An Invitation Sunday is not our preferred medium for mission"

This response always makes me want to ask the church leader what their preferred medium for mission is! Perhaps it is one where there is less chance for people to say "no".

There is a story from the Bible that is helpful with disciplining our disappointment. It is the Parable of the Sower. The Sower sows the seed. Some seed falls on the path and the birds come and eat it. You might say that's not fair, but the Bible says the Sower kept on sowing. Some of the seed fell on rocky ground and soon, as it started to grow, the sun shrivelled it up. Again, you might say that's not fair, but the Bible just says the Sower kept on sowing. Some of the seed fell amongst thorns and eventually was choked to death. You might still say that's not fair. The Bible says the Sower kept on sowing. The secret of the Sower was that he kept on sowing, until eventually the seed landed on the good ground. We need to fight off discouragement and discipline our disappointment, and then we will eventually find the good ground.

Take a look at an apple tree. There might be five hundred apples on the tree, each with ten seeds. That's a lot of seeds. We might ask, "Why would you need so many seeds to grow just a few more trees?"

God has something to teach us here. Firstly, through the apple tree, He is telling us: "Most seeds never grow but they do accomplish something. So if you really want to make something happen, you had better try more than once."

45

All seeds accomplish something. Often God leads us to poor soil in order to draw us closer in relationship with Him. One of my friends is a wine writer and he says that some of the best wines in the world come from poor soil. Apparently grapevines need to be stressed to produce quality fruit. The poor soil encourages the roots to dig deeper for water and other nutrients. This could also be a parable for our relationship with God.[2]

3. "I am already doing my best! What more do they want?"

We really don't do failure as church leaders. This is often because our congregations don't allow us to fail and so we stop taking risks, or get defensive when anybody suggests that there might be an alternative way of seeing or doing something. This is one of the major blocks at leadership level and we can start to blame other people rather than taking responsibility ourselves.

4. "We are doing this every week"

This is often the cry of the larger, very busy church: "We are seeing new people every week." I would ask two questions: What is your congregation size? And how many new people are you seeing every week? It will probably be the case that over 90 per cent of the congregation are not inviting and there is plenty of room for more people!

5. "I am just too busy"

In all fairness, the church *is* very busy. We are busy doing good things. We are feeding the poor, we have acts of worship to put on, we have rotas to organize. In our individual lives we live at such a pace that we have no time. Here is a useful word: *posteriority*. It is a word that we all need to learn. Posteriority is the opposite of priority. Posteriority is the things we should do last or not at all. They might be good things, but they are not the priority.

In order to find time in our busy lives, we need to learn the Law of Posteriority.[3] We will never catch up with all the things we need to do if we don't. Therefore we need to set priorities and understand posteriorities. We need to recognize when the good things we do are squeezing out the God things we need to do. Could doing good be wrong?

6. "My people are tired of inviting once a year"

Once again the real reason here is that the last time this church leader did an Invitation Sunday, it didn't work. But it is hard to admit that, so we need to make up a reason. Now there is truth behind the thought of a tired church. It may be because we are doing lots of good things. But I suspect the real tiredness of which this church leader speaks is closer to home.

Locks at a senior level

At very senior leadership level the locks are more sophisticated and intellectual. They generally take the form of:

- "The trouble is that we are a secular society."
- 'We are a post-Christian society."
- "This is the last generation who will have any knowledge of church, therefore…"
- "We have a post-Christendom fringe."
- "We need an emerging church in a postmodern society."
- "I don't like your missiology."

I always want to stop senior leaders in the middle of these phrases and ask, "Is Christ alive and active and working in our nation, or not?" Senior leaders can't say no to that question. So what has "secular", "post-Christian", "post-Christendom", "postmodern" and "poor missiology" got to do with anything? On a Sunday we are happy to say and sing how great our God is, how He moves the mountains, but on the Monday we seem to discount Him and explain away His perceived lack of action to right wrongs in our society. Nothing is impossible with our God, and it seems to me that these phrases paralyse us; they demonstrate our lack of faith and send us scampering off in the wrong direction. When we speak about secularism and being postmodern, we are talking about culture. Culture is group-think. We need to challenge it and replace it with how God thinks.

The locks at senior level are serious because of the impact that senior church figures can have. They can act as gatekeepers to whole denominations or dioceses. As in the tale of the emperor's new clothes, everybody around might be able to see that the emperor is naked, but nobody dares to say it. Senior leaders need to be open to being wrong, and must allow those around them to question and query their beliefs and theories freely. It is easy to start propagating a theory and after a while we can persuade ourselves it is true. Often we need those around us to help us spot the planks and splinters in our own eyes.

One day I was due to speak at a denominational business meeting. There was a lively debate to finish off the final agenda item before I spoke. The person responsible for finances stood up and announced that there was a proposal to increase by 4 per cent the amount of money paid by individual churches to the central body. A church leader then stood up and reacted angrily, saying that was ridiculous. The person responsible for finances said to the meeting, "Well, you have two options. Option one is to increase the amount of money paid to the central body. Option two is to cut down the number of church leaders." The chair of the meeting then brought the debate to a close and moved on to introduce me, explaining that I was there to talk about unlocking the growth.

The tactic of either cutting budgets or going on stewardship campaigns to raise additional income misses the nature of the challenges facing the church today. Our thought processes are often shaped around what we know we know, rather than what we don't know we don't know.

So I couldn't resist asking when I stood up, "What do you mean, there are only two options?" This thinking is prevalent across all our Christian denominations at the moment. We have lost confidence that we can grow, so instead we carefully manage decline.

Another lock for senior leaders is disillusionment, which says, "I have worked for over a decade in senior leadership at this level and have come to the conclusion that I can change very little."

The "nothing will ever change" lock is more prevalent than we would imagine at senior level. You'd think that a senior church leader would be able to make changes, but often the system of thought or the culture of "how we do things around here" is very hard to counteract, however senior you are. But the lock can be, and has to be, challenged. In writing for the second time to the church at Corinth, Paul says, "bringing into captivity every thought to the obedience of Christ" (2 Corinthians 10:5, KJV). Good advice for first-century and twenty-first-century Christians! We don't have to be a victim of our own thoughts.

As I have travelled through countries in the Western world which are overwhelmingly Christian, the most obvious lock I've encountered is the grip of discouragement and lack of belief. Discouragement is a besetting sin – one which constantly recurs – which contains elements of failure, shame and hopelessness. It is deeply ingrained in leadership at all levels in the church. Leaders don't reach into the future because they are trapped by the regret of the past – past failures, past mistakes – or they are so burdened by the routine of the present that they don't give enough thought to designing the future.

All these reasons become curses around our necks and paralyse and debilitate the church we love and our Christian lives, often without us knowing it. So in order to disguise this, we construct a new way of looking at life, which goes like this: "It was quite crowded in church tonight."

We invent a new semi-reality – the pretence that everything is not so bad under the circumstances. But perhaps until we repent of our ungodly reasons, thoughts, theories and beliefs, the blessing of God will be withheld. God is able to bypass all sorts of rubbish, but He gives us free will to decide how we live our lives, and when we decide not to do something, He will not force us to do what is right.

When was the last time that invitation was an item on the senior management or leadership agenda at your church? Invitation is right in the middle of mission. In fact, in most of the mission initiatives, invitation plays a major part. Yet we have had a problem with invitation for decades, one we have just ignored up until now. Surely it is worth taking time out to pause and reflect on it. Just raising awareness, and teaching into some of these locks, can dramatically increase the numbers of people being invited on a yearly basis.

Questions to think about

Firstly, ask your church leadership: "What stops our congregation inviting their friends?" Then put the same question to your congregation. From the answers, identify the locks. Address the locks with good teaching, and replace them with godly thinking.

Here are some questions to help you to teach into the locks:

1. How can we invite when we are rubbish at inviting?

2. How can we invite when we all suffer during our act of worship?

3. How can we invite when we are still disappointed about the last person who said "no" to us?

4. How can we invite when we have no friends?

5. How can we invite when we are reticent/shy?

6. How can we invite when our services and people are unpredictable?

7. How can we invite when we fear rejection?

Underneath all seven of these questions, which could form the basis for sermons, is *fear*. Whatever the mountain of fear we are facing, we are told to say to it, "Go, throw yourself into the sea" (Mark 11:23). Fear is the most destructive element of the human personality and is an enemy to the Christian. This is why we are told, "Do not be afraid" (John 14:27). Imagination is a source of fear but it could also be the solution. Romans 8:31 says, "If God is for us, who can be against us?" If we fill our minds with the fact that God is for us, we can defeat fear. When our minds are full of God, there is no room for worry and anxiety over the response to an invitation. God has given the solution to fear within us. We may need to start with faith the size of a mustard seed. But even that is big enough as we face the fear. Small faith will give you small results, but it will move you in the right direction and sooner or later you will have medium faith giving medium results, which can then lead to bigger faith giving bigger results. We can use the fear to actually build a deeper relationship with God. God has laid within us, through the power of the Holy Spirit, all the potential we need to lead a constructive life of faith. But teaching will not be enough. The economist J. K. Galbraith once observed: "Faced with the choice between changing one's mind and proving that there is no need to do so, almost everyone gets busy on the proof"[4]

We spend so much time renovating and refurbishing our church buildings. What we really need to do is to be constantly refurbishing our minds. Beating the culture of fear will be an ongoing battle to be joined on a regular basis by church leaders and their leadership teams.

Underlying all these sermon topics is the real issue which stops people in your church inviting friends, and which is the key to mobilizing invitation: that is, admitting there is a problem and asking for forgiveness – forgiveness for not doing the things we ought to be doing. My experience says that if we do not ask for forgiveness the impact of our invitation will be limited. But at the moment we don't even recognize that we aren't inviting, and that is something that needs to be repented, urgently.

Secondly, during my seminars I ask the question, "Who invited you and how were you first invited to church?"

This is another major discovery tool for helping congregations to unlock the invitational culture. Many congregational members will not even think that they have been invited. Many of us consider ourselves as cradle Christians – or neonatal Christians, responding in the womb to the act of worship! However, we *were* invited – by our parents. Many parents today have not invited their children to church, but their parents invited them. Once we understand that we have been blessed through invitation, perhaps we may pass on the blessing of our invitation in the remaining years of our life.

The answers to "Who invited you?" are so varied that I can't help but picture God planning the myriad ways in which He is going to help us connect with His people. Here are just a few of the reasons I have heard for saying "yes" to going to church – in no particular order. Not all are as worthy as the others!

- Attraction: "There was a gorgeous girl/boy and I knew I would have to go to church to have any chance of going out with her/him!"

- Being conned: "I was invited to a supper only to find out that it was a church event."

- Football: "The church had a football team and I had to go to church in order to play."

- Being good at singing: "I was told that the church choir was in desperate need of a soprano for a short period of time!"

- Uniformed organizations: "I was marched into church with the Scouts!"

- The children: "It was time to take my children to church, as I had once been taken."

A final thought: Who invited you to church? Please write a letter to them to thank them (even if it was your parents!).

Chapter 3

How Welcoming Are You?

I have never met anyone who admits to going to an unwelcoming church, yet we all know that there are some unwelcoming churches out there. In fact, I believe that Christian churches are institutionally unwelcoming. Now you might be reading this thinking, "Well, my church is welcoming, thank you very much." But come on a journey with me, back to some of the church welcomes I've experienced, and then see if you really think your church is welcoming.

Are you a guest or a host in the church to which you belong? There is a big difference between the two roles. If I came to your home I would be the guest and you would be the host. You would make sure that I felt welcome; perhaps you'd offer me a cup of coffee and ask if I needed anything to eat. Now fast forward this guest-and-host principle to church. Could you be sure, on this coming Sunday, that any stranger could walk into your church building and be well hosted by any regular member of the congregation? I don't just mean the Welcome Team, but any member of the congregation. Do you remember being welcomed into your church?

I was on tour in North America and wanted to find a church to attend on Sunday morning. I gave a friend a description of the kind of church I'd like to go to, somewhere where I could experience a good teacher and somewhere with uplifting musical worship. My friend suggested a couple of churches, one with a gifted Bible teacher and another with wonderful musical worship, and said that I could make both services because one started at 9 a.m. and the other at 11 a.m., and there was just a ten-minute walk between the two churches. I went to the first service; there were 500 people present and the preaching was inspiring. Then I walked the ten minutes to the second service, which was also attended by 500 people, and the musical worship was uplifting. However, in the whole morning, in both churches, I was spoken to just once and it happened like this.

In the second service the leader asked the congregation to "turn to the person next to you and introduce yourself". Why this phrase was not contained in the writings of the apostle Paul I don't know, because it gets repeated more times than certain passages of Scripture! (By the way, what does it say that the service leader was so confident that this had not already been done?) So I turned and spoke to the young man next to me and introduced myself. I told him why I was in the country and he told me a little about the church. The leader of the service then brought us back to the act of worship. That was the only time in both services that someone spoke to me and it only happened because people were ordered to do so! I attended coffee after each of the acts of worship and hung around a bit, but nobody approached me. On the way out of the second church I noticed a welcome desk, so I went up to the desk, placed my hand on it and said, "Thank you for welcoming me." You see, if we are not going to have a congregation of hosts, we might as well get a welcome desk!

So are we guests or hosts in our congregations? We could have been in our church congregation for five, ten, fifteen, twenty years and still be acting as a guest. I think the idea of personal Christianity has gone far too far. I would call it selfish Christianity, as it always seems to be about me. "Was the sermon any good for me today? Did the songs make me feel better about myself?" What happened to the idea of the body of Christ and that we are all part of one body? Do we in our churches know how to act as hosts or are we only interested in being a guest?[1]

I have heard it said that visitors coming to church decide in the first thirty seconds whether they will ever return. So how should we manage those first thirty seconds? Let me show you how, all too often, we do manage it. We rota it! We ask for volunteers with a pulse. We call it a duty, when it is really a ministry. One person told me how a church member said to her, on finding out that she was new and hearing her story of being poorly welcomed, "I would have welcomed you but I wasn't on duty that Sunday!"

In terms of welcome, some people need to be under-welcomed, whilst others need to be over-welcomed, but to know the difference between the two and all the variations in between, needs people who have wonderful personal skills. However, as in many areas of church life, we settle for second best and ask for volunteers, instead of identifying the great welcomers we have among us and setting them free into their ministry. You see, if you have a rota system, it is very difficult to know if someone is new or has been coming for a few weeks if you have not been on duty yourself. I know someone who used to work in a very chic restaurant and every day they prepared the staff extensively for that evening by giving them information about who was due to dine, how often they had been before and how the serving staff might be able to offer a personalized welcome. Our churches could learn a lot from restaurants! We need to change our thinking and then our practice in this area. In the twelve steps (see Chapter 4) and the ten keys (see Chapter 9) I set out some practical suggestions on how to do this.

Sadly, things can get even worse for our newcomer than just being ignored, because often we manage to appoint the grumpiest people on our duty rota, those who just shove books in people's hands and grunt at them. Parents know that they can have a wonderful conversation with their sons up to the age of 12 years and 364 days, but on that 365th day something strange happens and normal conversation turns into monosyllabic answers, if you are lucky. Some of our greeters appear to revert to teenagers when they are on welcome duty; they become incapable of holding any conversation or offering a wonderful welcome. Some church leaders have told me that their church uses the greeters' rota, in order to encourage attendance from that person. And I've actually seen how in some places people only turn up if they are on a rota. The crazy world of church!

Some newcomers have to put up with a "self-service" welcome. This is when they turn up twenty minutes early or arrive ten minutes late. I have heard from church leaders that as they are ten minutes into the act of worship, they see the new visitor at the back of the church, trying to work out which books they need to pick up, and craning their necks to see where they can sit. This happens because the greeters have finished their duty and are now blissfully unaware of the newcomers. The leader then desperately attempts to convey the following message to the greeters without saying a word: "Will somebody just get up and help the person at the back of the church?"

I know that many churches do now have a Welcome Team, furnished with badges to make it easy for visitors to remember names, but for the most part these people are still on a rota, as church leaders feel they cannot possibly ask the same people to do this "duty" every single week. The thinking goes, how could people possibly enjoy church if they had to do that duty every week?

Now, I would be hopeless on a Welcome Team, because when I hear names they enter through one ear and escape through the other. It is so embarrassing when you have no system for remembering names. There is one man in my church who has told me his name and I should really go up to him and say, "Sorry, what's your name again?" But I have known him so long, I don't dare to! So don't rota me for the Welcome Team! Instead, use the people who do have these skills and will delight in having them recognized and used.

Somebody once said to me that Back to Church Sunday should be renamed "Back of Church Sunday". In a theatre the most expensive tickets are for seats near the front, but when you go to church, the seats fill up from the back. You can put out two rows of chairs in any church and you know that the back row will always be taken first, just as summer follows spring. There may be a number of reasons for this phenomenon. Perhaps those on the back row enjoy keeping an eye on things and arrive early to grab the best seats. And nobody wants to sit on the front row in case they appear too enthusiastic. Many church leaders see gaping rows of empty seats at the front, while most of the congregation sit towards the back of the church building. But because all the seats at the back are taken, first-time visitors, who generally want to blend in, are forced to walk up the aisle (known by some church leaders as "the walk of doom"!) past filled seat after filled seat, until they find the empty spaces at the front.

If you are new and you have to sit on the front row, it makes it harder to follow the service as there is no one in front to guide you. Someone once suggested to me that you need wing-mirrors to see when to sit and when to stand.

So, if we imagine our newcomers have already been embarrassed by having to march to the front, and if we can make them trip over a few handbags and force them to climb over church members who conveniently sit at the end of the pews for an early escape, then we can almost be certain we'll never see them again. To try to avoid this, perhaps we should announce that the front two rows will be a collection-free zone and see if they fill up more quickly?

Newcomers to many of our historic churches still have to negotiate the intricate politics of the pew system. We may not pay for our pews any longer, but we are all guilty of feeling that sense of betrayal if our normal position in the church building has been taken by somebody else. I always make the mistake of sitting in the congregation if I go to a church to preach. There is plenty of space with five minutes to go, but then with one minute to go the family of five come ambling down the aisle and stare in horror at the sight before them. Someone (i.e. me) has taken their pew! After moments of indecision they either try their best to reclaim their space by squeezing past or, in not completely silent protest, sit behind, unable to enjoy the act of worship that week, mentally preparing the note they will send to the church leader about the incident. By the way, don't think that by removing the pews all will be well. People are like homing pigeons in terms of church seating. They will always find their nest and then protect it from strangers. One bishop told me that he was sitting in the congregation awaiting the start of the service, with his head bowed in prayer, when he felt a tap on his shoulder followed by the words, "You're in my seat." He raised his head and heard the lady exclaim, "Oh no – it's the Bishop!"

I always thought that we could send a photographer

into the same church on two consecutive Sundays and have him or her take a photo of the congregation on both days. Then you could have a "spot the difference" competition! But somebody recently pointed out to me that as many attenders think regular attendance is once a month, it wouldn't work.

After the service, we have another chance to make people feel really welcome in the post-service coffee time. This is the time when newcomers can really get to know the congregation – or at least that's the idea, isn't it? I don't think so! This is often the time for newcomers to be studiously ignored. I was told that one church had a tradition that any unused mug at coffee time was known as a "Thank God" – as in, "We thank God for the cups and saucers not used"! Is there a better example of a church cursing itself into closure?

What does welcome actually look like? Would you invite someone to your home, speak to them for an hour, and then offer them coffee on the way out? I am not suggesting that we need coffee before the service (though strong caffeine would keep more of us awake), but it's a good idea to try to understand what welcome might look like if we started with a blank sheet of paper. I got into big trouble once by introducing an idea called "Doughnut Sunday" at the church I attend. Every fifth Sunday I went and bought trays of doughnuts; we announced this and people started bringing their friends, particularly children. All was going well until some of the jam from the doughnuts escaped and made a break for freedom on the church carpet, and before anyone could send for a senior church leader to resolve the matter,

about church the building, church the act of worship, or church as the people of God? Signs like this can confirm in people's minds that they have to have their whole life in order before they are able to come, that they don't belong there. I have heard many people who have made steps towards church say that they felt hypocritical about coming, as their lives did not match up to their image of a church person. (Five minutes among most of our congregations would dismiss that thought from their minds!) We have almost created a church ghetto separated from our communities. We need to pay attention to the messages our signs are sending out to people. Sometimes some of our signs lower people's expectations of the church. Some people's expectations are so low that they are pleasantly surprised when they do pay us a visit!

But if we assume that the first-time visitor has finally got comfortable and has been greeted well, what happens to them then? They now have to tackle the impenetrable language of the church, whether that is just the assumption that everyone knows what is going on, or the general lack of appreciation that there might be anyone new in the congregation. It is no longer in Latin, but sometimes it may as well be.

It feels awful if you are fumbling through multiple books, not knowing where you are meant to be, so on people's first visit we need to be aware of this and give extra guidance from the front.

Questions to think about

After reading this chapter, would you still say your church is welcoming? Or would you admit that we are all in churches where welcome can be improved? A good exercise for a leadership team is to regularly review welcome by asking four simple questions:

• What does our welcome look like before the service?

• What does our welcome look like during the service?

• What does our welcome look like after the service?

• What does our welcome look like after Sunday?

You may wish to sign up a mystery worshipper on a six-monthly basis, to give you an independent perspective as well. And don't forget to ask, on a scale of one to ten, would your first timers recommend your church to their friends and family?

Chapter 4
Twelve Steps to Becoming an Inviting Church

In the early years of the Back to Church Sunday initiative, I was aware that many church leaders had tried it once and because they didn't get a boost to their numbers, they decided that it didn't work and they'd give it a miss the following year. In year two there is also a general trend for the results to go down and churches do often drop away. So although the concept of having an Invitation Sunday on a set day in September each year grew and grew to include over 6,000 churches, its growth masked these disappointing figures.

One day I finally woke up to the issue and wrote to some of those church leaders I'd worked with closely across the UK and said that I wanted to find people who had tried an Invitation Sunday but for whom it hadn't worked, because I wanted to work with them on doubling their congregation in a day. I sent the email and almost immediately regretted it because I wasn't sure I did know how to double a congregation in a day. Fortunately I wasn't knocked over in the rush to join up! But eventually twenty-five church leaders came forward. My idea was to have four ten-minute phone calls with each leader in the run-up to an Invitation Sunday. There would be one call in June, one in July, one in August, and one in September. On the evening before the first call I was panicking and regretting my big mouth, wondering what on earth I was going to say. But I then remembered this poem called "Belief System", possibly by Charles Reade:

> *If you accept a belief,*
> *You reap a thought.*
> *If you sow a thought,*
> *You reap an attitude.*
> *If you sow an attitude,*
> *You reap an action.*
> *If you sow an action,*
> *You reap a habit.*
> *If you sow a habit,*
> *You reap a character.*
> *If you sow a character,*
> *You reap a destiny.*[1]

I was fascinated by the word "habit". I looked up its meaning in a dictionary and it described "habit" as "an acquired pattern of behaviour that happens automatically". The English poet John Dryden said, "We first make our habits, then our habits make us."[2] Though most of us don't like to admit to it, we are all creatures of habit. But at the moment our churches are not in the habit of inviting people.

I was drinking a glass of red wine and searching the internet for instances mentioning the word "habit", when I came across the Alcoholics Anonymous website. (It has been suggested to me that perhaps God was speaking about the red wine!) The website offered a twelve-step process for kicking the habit. It made me wonder whether there could be a twelve-step process for kicking the habit of being an uninviting church. I scribbled down what I thought these twelve steps might be and went to sleep confidently knowing I had something to share with the church leaders.

The "Belief System" poem teaches us that we can alter our destiny by altering our thoughts, and the twelve steps are a way of encouraging the church to move into invitational mission.

But it is important to note that the twelve steps are a strategy, and "Culture eats strategy for breakfast"![3] This explains why focused Invitation Sundays have not worked for many churches. A church may have a strategy which includes a leader enthusiastically recommending that the congregation should invite their friends, family or neighbours to church, but in the event very few church members may actually do so.

Over the years, churches have had initiative after initiative with this strategy of encouraging invitation to some event or other, and yet sometimes the strategy bears little or no fruit.

The issue is that "culture eats strategy for breakfast". Culture tells us how we do things around here and we stick to it. Frankly, also, we are a generation of Christians that has not had the practice of invitation. We have to work out why the congregation are not inviting their friends or are not going to invite their friends. This is what I call "disturbing the ground". Before a farmer goes to sow the seed, he will take a tractor and plough up the ground. Unless this is done effectively the seed will not be planted properly. The way we think in church right now is the ground. We need to disturb the way we are thinking by turning the soil over. This allows the possibility for good thinking to be planted.

Unless we do this important piece of work, all the strategy of enthusiastic invitation will just be consumed by the present culture which fears and resists invitation.

I once asked someone at a seminar why she didn't ever invite. After freezing for half a minute she said that it just didn't feel right. She is not alone in being frozen by fear. It is not the failure which is holding us back; it is the anticipation of rejection.

Timidity is an affliction that can be cured, but it needs to be recognized as a problem first. The best place to start is with an "I am sorry", as in "Our name is [insert the name of your church] and we are not an inviting church." We can then enter our own twelve-step programme. Dramatic changes could follow.

Here are the twelve steps I came up with that night. I've fine-tuned them since:

Step 1: Vision

Does your fig tree have figs? Does your ministry have fruit? Are you extending God's kingdom year by year?

I have seen churches double their congregations in a day and retain 10 per cent the following Sunday by adopting a vision of high expectations. This is the first of three key steps to increasing your congregation and helping to disciple your present congregation through a simple invitation to invite.

I always ask church leaders when I speak to them: "Would you go in front of your congregation and say something like this: 'If every one of us invited a friend and they accepted, we would double our congregation. Let's do it!'?"

Now at this point many people will usually say exactly why this won't work, because our tendency is to measure any new idea by the life that we know. But if we are not careful, all our decisions will be ruled by our past experiences. We need to rethink what is possible. Here are just some of the reasons offered by people who aren't willing to give invitation another chance:

- "My people are all elderly and all their friends are in the congregation anyway."

- "We've tried this before."

- "We're no good at inviting people."

These thoughts are only our destiny if we decide we want them to be our destiny. We need to expand our vision of ourselves, let our imagination run free, instead of letting our past dictate our future. Nothing is impossible for God!

But hearing from people why they think it won't work has its uses; it helps identify the locks in their minds on success. Then people can be helped to accept that these locks need not be their destiny unless they decide they want them to be their destiny.

Each negative thought needs to be replaced by a more empowering one, like:

- "We are going to learn how to invite."

- "We are going to ask God to show us *how* to invite."

- "We are going to ask God *who* to invite."

Of course, often these locks are like the planks in our eyes: only others can see them.

We can all preach about vision. As the prophet Nathan said to King David, "Whatever you have in *mind* [my emphasis], go ahead and do it, for the Lord is with you" (2 Samuel 7:3). An invitation is an opportunity to put vision into practice and at the same time put your reputation and career on the line!

But whether you think you can or think you can't, what you decide about yourself will determine what happens. Do we believe that the Lord is with us? Sadly, I think we in the church sometimes proclaim that God is everywhere, while we live as if He is really nowhere. But God is here with us. I believe God has been speaking throughout the writing of this book and is speaking as you read it (see Psalm 139:7–10).

I could write a whole book on the psychosomatic church. We are all familiar with psychosomatic illness – an illness that has physical symptoms, but whose origin is in the mind and emotions. The mind tells the body it is ill because the mind is struggling to cope. It is the mind's way of telling the individual that there is a problem and it needs to be addressed.

Why the psychosomatic church? The controlling mind is the church leadership and the body is the people of God. If the controlling mind sends distress signals to the body, then it is likely that the body will not be healthy. The symptoms of this illness might be:

- Lack of expectation.

- Nice-ianity rather than Christianity.

- Club 65–85.

- Mission the preoccupation of the few.

- Over-concentration on acts of worship.

- Busy doing good.

I gave examples earlier of a number of conversations with senior leaders over the years which have led to questions such as: "How do you see the future for the church?" Frequently I receive answers such as: "Well, we are in a secular society" or "We are in a post-Christian society". Words such as these, which are sent to and heard by the "body" of the church, have a debilitating impact.

There are locks at every level of the church: at

congregational level, including those not yet worshipping with us; at church leadership level; and at very senior level, where the locks tend to be more intellectual, and have been honed and practised to such a degree that nearly everyone takes them as gospel truth. It is not a question of whether people believe, but it is a lack of expectancy that God is going to do anything, because our generation of Christian leaders have had to deal with constant decline. It is hard to imagine people queuing outside church buildings, hoping to get a seat for the act of worship. We have no experience of this happening. So instead of working in expectation of it, we concentrate on managing resources well and trying to make the money go further. We develop our muscles only to manage decline.

The psychosomatic church is unfortunately alive and kicking. We need to understand and challenge its culture, and then set a vision to move in the opposite direction.

Have you heard the old story of the chicken and the pig walking down a country road early in the morning, getting more and more hungry? Then they come across a place that has a sign that says, "Breakfast – Eggs and Bacon". The chicken gets all puffed up, saying, "What would the breakfast be without my contribution?" The pig says, "It's OK for you! For you it's a contribution, but for me it's total commitment!"

Now some people have said to me, "Why do we have to set a vision and see it achieved in a set timescale?" Setting a timescale is important. Jesus taught us about this in the story of the master and the servants in the parable of the talents (Matthew 25:14–30). The master said to the servants, "How did you do in the allotted time I gave you?" A very important question! In the King James Bible it says the master "reckoneth" with the servants – there was a reckoning. The first servant said, "I turned five talents into ten." Now, do you think there is a significance in the doubling from five to ten? Should we be expecting doubling in a reasonable timescale? Shouldn't we be expected to make progress? The second servant said, "I turned two talents into four." Do you think there is a significance again here in the doubling? If we have a lot of time, if we have no deadline, there is a danger that everything can drift off track, which is why short timescales are good.

But what should be our proper response when we don't get results? The master was furious with the servant who was given one talent and hid it. Does the fig tree have any figs? It seems that fig trees better have figs when the maker of the fig tree comes by!

So setting a vision and committing to this vision is really important. "Without vision the people perish" – the body dies. Many church leaders fail with their congregations not because they aim too high and miss, but because they aim too low, or don't even aim at all.

Some tips for setting a vision include:

- Think big in the vision you want to achieve.

- Believe that God has given you authority to move (try to think of yourself as God thinks of you).

- Share the vision.

- Go and make it happen.

- Focus (on the thing that it is absolutely important).

- Never give up (just because it gets hard).

We need to hold in balance the expectation that God wants to double our congregation in a day with the understanding that sometimes God wants to bless us through a different response. For most of us the skill and practice of expectation has either been stolen or damaged by years of discouragement, disappointment, unbelief, poor self-esteem, or half truths we've accepted as whole ones. To set a goal to double a congregation in a day is valuable not for the goal itself, but for what it will make of you to achieve it, for the person you will have to become to achieve it.

But in the end, is your vision inevitable? Are you going to do the work to make it happen in your church, to bring it to fruition? If not, you are not really committed and you won't be able to do this.

Step 2: Modelling

Now, by this I don't mean getting some of our church leaders modelling on the catwalk! What I mean is that church leaders come to me and say, "Back to Church Sunday is a waste of time", and I say, "I'm sorry. What was the problem?" They say, "Nobody invited anyone." At this point I usually ask, gently, "Well, did you invite someone?"

This is what modelling sounds like when you are a church leader: "I am inviting someone. Will you?" We should rarely ask our congregations to do something that we are not prepared to do ourselves. We need to "be the change we want to see in others", as Gandhi famously put it. The only things that we can control as a leader are inviting the congregation to invite, and then issuing our own invitation to a friend, or friends. What we cannot control is whether our congregation will follow through or whether our friends will accept an invitation. But we can model the process, even if our invitee says no. We affirm the invitation, not the answer to the invitation.

Church leaders need to lead by example, to "walk the talk".

In the gospels Jesus models the behaviour His disciples will follow. In the gospel of John, Philip will make the same three-word invitation to Nathanael that was given to him, that had been given to Andrew. The first thing we can do, then, is to model the behaviour we hope our people will adopt.

Now one of the modern miracles is that as soon as a church leader steps out and models and sets the vision by saying something like, "If every one of us invited a friend and they accepted, we would double our congregation. So let's do it! In fact, I'm inviting someone. Will you?" – as soon as that happens, 20 per cent of the congregation will immediately know who they are going to invite. Now this is a miracle, as they probably have not invited a friend to the church service with them that week. All it takes for them to do so now is a bit of vision and modelling. The greatest leadership is by example.

But the bad news is that, despite you as a church leader stepping out in faith and asking for a doubling of your congregation, 80 per cent of your congregation are still just not going to participate. Why not? Well, when you say: "If every one of us invited a friend and they accepted, we would double our congregation. So let's do it! In fact, I'm inviting someone. Will you?" – 80 per cent of your congregation are thinking to themselves: "They don't mean me, they mean the people who are really involved in this congregation – not me."

Now this is a very convenient thought for members of the congregation to have, as we saw in Chapter 2 when we looked at the reasons why Christians don't invite their friends. So what you need to do is to follow Step 3.

Step 3: Cascading

Cascading is making sure that every single person in a congregation is "personally" invited to invite. I call this the exponential growth step, or we could call it the discipling step. This is the step all ordained people have in their original call from God. That call consists of coming alongside individual people and helping them in their faith journey. It is a very powerful step.

You have to take invitation down to a one-on-one level. We often assume, wrongly, that by talking to a lot of people, they will have all heard the things that have been said. We might think they heard our call to invite, but in fact, for around 80 per cent it has gone straight over their heads. So what we have to do is personally invite people to invite. Now I can hear the howls of protest at that suggestion! There must a less time-consuming way, surely? If you have multiple congregations or a large congregation, how can you possibly make this happen? The leader of a church of over 1,000 in north-west England comments:

The whole process was an interesting one for me. I realized that despite having a clear plan over four weeks, when you delegate the communication of something to others the level of briefing needed to get the content, tone and clarity that you want is actually massive. On one or two occasions the communication from the front was not as good as I would have wanted, but it was ten times better than we would have done before.

First, personal invitation is better than any other form of invitation. For example, if you wanted to find a Sunday school teacher for your teenage class, you have three ways of going about this task. First, you could put a notice in the church notice-sheet, probably for several consecutive weeks. Second, you could make sure it was promoted in the notices said each week at the front of church. Or third, you could ask God who He might want you to ask and then go and ask that person personally. Now, the third way will not automatically result in success, but it is more likely to do so than the other two ways. I am not against vision from the front of church or notices in the notice-sheet, but on their own they are still not as effective as a personal invitation. They may be more efficient, but they are not as effective.

The church leader needs to take the vision and make it personal, by going up to individual members of the congregation and inviting them to invite. Even after this, some people may still not invite, but they are more likely to. Now, how do you cascade in a large church or across multiple congregations? I think this strikes at the heart of what is church – a question that I will attempt to address in chapter eight. How about sharing your vision personally with a group of people who can then make sure that every member of the congregation is asked to invite someone? One way not to do it is to announce it from the front, asking people to turn to the person next to them and to ask them who they are inviting; or to hand out cards as people are in a line leaving church. Someone once said: "There are no exceptions to the rule that everybody likes to be an exception to the rule." In other words, everyone wants to be seen as special, which is how God sees us, and if we attempt to reach people by lumping them all together we are probably not reaching them at all.

On a car journey into the Australian outback my driving companion introduced me to the phrase, "shortcuts cause erosion". This phrase got me thinking about the shortcuts we have taken in how we disciple today. In church at the moment we prefer efficient leadership to effective leadership. Cascading takes us into effective leadership. The leadership of our churches often takes a shortcut in discipleship, thinking that a sermon on a Sunday morning to a congregation is good enough, when actually it often isn't. This approach has caused an erosion in what it means to be a Christian disciple. Jesus spent a lot of time in a one-to-twelve situation as well as a lot of one-on-one discipling. Vision and modelling often need to be taken to a one-on-one level.

Most members of a congregation have limited contact with the church leadership. Sometimes it can feel as if it takes illness to get maximum attention from church leadership. So imagine if the leader or someone from the leadership team actually asks you to do something. Apart from fainting in shock, most of us would be likely to do all we could to try to fulfil the request. Some of us would be mortified, of course, but we'd still secretly be pleased to be asked. The key to mobilizing the whole congregation is in the power of one on one. We need to make congregational members feel as important as they are to God. We need to build the self-esteem of the congregation, that they are indeed ambassadors for Christ.

One of the fall-outs of an Invitation Sunday is that some congregational members will stay away on that Sunday because they have either been turned down by a friend or they have not plucked up the courage to ask anyone and so are embarrassed to turn up alone. This is very sad, and even more so as it means that if we have brought a friend along to church there are fewer people to introduce them to afterwards. We can try to prevent this by reminding people (and ourselves) that success is in the invitation, not the answer.

Now, one of the marvellous side-effects of modelling and cascading is that it offers a safety net for congregational members, because if the church leader personally invites a member to invite, they can then say to their friend that the leader has asked them to do it.

It goes like this: "I didn't want to invite you, but they made me do it!"

The importance of the church leader personally inviting congregational members is that the member can blame the leader! To overcome the fear of invitation, a church leader needs broad shoulders to take all that blame, but it is well worthwhile.

If you don't do anything else, make sure you set vision, model vision, and cascade vision one to one.

Step 4: The gift of friendship

Many of us see friendship as ordinary, but friendship is extraordinary. You can't be friends with everybody but there are some people who you are immediately drawn towards. It can be incredible when you connect with someone for the first time, and a deep friendship takes place. With a close friend, you might not have spoken to them for a year, but you can pick up the phone immediately after reading this sentence, and it will be as if you spoke to them yesterday. There is a real spiritual connection.

We need to get over our current pseudo-magnanimous attitude of not wanting to put our friend through the trial of church and trust that our connection will remain strong, whatever they think of our church.

Think about it: wouldn't you do most things your best friend asked, if you possibly could? For example, if my friend asked me whether I would like to go to the ballet with him, my first reaction might be "You must be joking!" Then my friend might say that he has a spare ticket, and I would say, "I'm not surprised!" But in the end I would go to the ballet with him, not because I wanted to go to the ballet, but because my friend had asked me to go. We mustn't think that when we invite our friends to church they are coming purely for the act of worship. They are coming primarily because you asked them to come. But when your friend says yes, at that moment the verse, "where two or three come together in my name, there am I with them" (Matthew 18:20) is very appropriate, and that invitation and its acceptance take the friendship on to a different, deeper level.

We need more teaching on friendship and the spiritual connection between friends. For example, I am fascinated by the phrases "de-churched" and "un-churched" which have come into the common language of our church life. The term de-churched seems to mean those who have left mainstream acts of worship, and the term un-churched refers to those who have never had any associations with the church in any form. But mightn't God have a different definition of the church, which is His people scattered throughout the world connecting with others through friendship? Friendship is an area to explore in terms of the church's mission to the world.

Step 5: The power of story

In many of our denominations it might take a liturgical commission sitting for fifteen years to get modern stories into our acts of worship. For other, non-liturgical churches story or testimony is only there for special occasions. We read stories every week from the gospels, from the New and Old Testaments, but our most recent stories are left out. Did story end with the gospels or is God still doing things through story today?

In my seminars I normally ask, "When you first came into a church setting, who invited you?" Over the many seminars I have led, I have heard some wonderful answers to this question. Very rarely are any of them what we would call "holy" or "spiritual". For example:

- "There was a gorgeous-looking girl I wanted to get to know, so I got myself invited."

- "My wife kept on at me to come."

- "The Scouts marched me into church."

- "My friend invited me."

- "My mother-in-law asked me."

- "It was through a choir member who knew I could sing."

- "God invited me" (perhaps this one is holy!)

I always try to ask, "And what was the name of the person who invited you?" In New Zealand I asked one young woman who had invited her, and the name of that person. She said that it was a girl who had invited her, but she couldn't remember her name. I went on with my seminar, until suddenly she remembered that her friend's name was "Precious". It took some time to come back to her, but when it did, the name had a great spiritual significance. If we ever get the chance to tell our faith story, very often we miss out the person who actually grasped the nettle and did the inviting in the first place. In fact these unsung people *are* precious – where would we be without them? We have been blessed by retelling our stories; now can we be a blessing to others? Telling our story gives courage to the story-teller and opens up possibilities for the listener.

Many of us currently in church feel we have never actually been invited. I've heard people say:

- "I cannot remember not being at church."

- "My mum and dad brought me."

- "I came as a babe in arms."

But when parents bring their children to church, there is still an implicit invitation. God invited some of us through our parents. Invitation has been part and parcel of how we got to be within the church setting.

I recommend again that, once you have worked out who invited you, you should write or phone to tell them what a blessing they have been in your own life. If that person is no longer alive, find a way of giving thanks for the life of Christ revealed through invitation in their lives.

We need to find time and space for stories – stories that inspire, stories that bring courage, stories that invite the next generation.

Step 6: Who has God been preparing in my life?

Either we accept that God is speaking to people today and preparing them for a relationship with Himself, or we think God is not! Many of us are like the boy Samuel. We do not recognize when God is speaking, but through invitation we can start to hear His prompting.

We need to connect with those God has been preparing for invitation in our lives. I often find that the first line of defence in any congregation when they are asked to think about inviting someone is that "All my friends are here already." Now if that is true, it should tell us something about how we need to live our lives. But we'll sidestep it for now by asking God who He has been preparing in our lives. If He does not tell us who He wants us to invite, then we are off the hook (for now)!

Asking gives us an opportunity to listen out for God speaking into our lives. The name might not come in the middle of the act of worship; it might come as you are working during the week, or exercising, or eating, or through silence, but I believe He is capable of letting us know who that person should be. Even if the person you ask says no, you have obeyed the instruction. One definition of true worship is obedience to the voice of God.

We need to be looking for the invitation of God in what He is about to do next.

When Jesus sent out the seventy-two mentioned in Luke's gospel, he taught us something very important about invitation (Luke 10:1–20).

There is a harvest

Time and again I hear the story of those who have been invited and are added to the church, who say that they were just waiting for the invitation.

Jesus is Lord of the harvest

Christ is active and working in our nations today, preparing people for the church to invite so that the kingdom of God might be extended.

There are people of peace

There is a seeking for the spiritual in our society, and as we go and invite we will meet people who are absolutely open to help us.

There will be rejection

Remember: they do not reject you, they reject Christ and the one who sent Christ. Some people will say yes, some people will say no. We have to get used to this and not let it put us off inviting.

You will have authority

We are seeing hundreds of thousands of accepted invitations across our nations. One word of open-handed invitation from a Christian can totally change the course of a person's life.

Step 7: Practise the question

Practise the nine words that can change a life. Step 7 is not intellectually challenging, or going to cost your church hundreds of thousands of pounds to implement. There is no long training course in order to practise the answer to every conceivable question anybody could ask and be so scared off by the end that we never put into practice what we have learnt.

No. The question is only this: "Would… you… like… to… come… to… church… with… me?"

We could, of course, have a training evening but it would last less than ten seconds. The beauty of this question is that anybody could ask it. There is no discrimination in the spirituality of invitation. Everybody can take part.

There are some more difficult questions out there, such as "Could you start using deodorant?" or "Will you marry me?" But this isn't one of them. (Although some of us might say that "Would you like to come to church with me?" is on a par with those questions!) However, at the end of the day, the person we are asking can answer in two ways: "Yes" or "No". If they say "No", don't dwell on it, pray on it!

The psychology of invitation is fascinating. Many

boys have sleepless nights before approaching the girl they want to invite out. It is not the difficulty of the task but the enormity of the moment that strikes fear into their hearts. Whether a young man asks a girl out for the first time or a Christian invites their friend to church, the palpitations are the same! Can we hold our nerve? When we invite someone to something which doesn't matter very much to us, we don't feel so nervous, but as soon as it means everything, then our resolve wobbles.

Some of us might just say here, "What's the problem? Ask the question and just move on!" Neuroscientists have discovered something they describe as expert-induced amnesia. When you have had hundreds of hours of practice at boldly inviting people to do something, you can invite without even knowing how you do it. Invitation rookies, however, are like learner drivers: they are focusing on every aspect of the process. We all know, though, that after a few months of driving, we drive without consciously monitoring every move as we did as a learner. So practice is essential.

I have been told, usually by those who mean very well, that we should leave all mission to the specialists, the evangelists, those with gifts in this area. Ordinary mortals are too shy or just not good at it!

But it is precisely this kind of thinking that has made mission the preoccupation of the few. Not many of us will feel utterly confident in this area (I know that I don't), but practice makes perfect. The more we do something and stretch ourselves, the easier it becomes. I have been rejected thousands of times, but the more I ask the less fearful I become. In the end it becomes a natural part of my life. In fact it becomes an unconscious habit.

There was nothing intellectually challenging when Jesus said, "Follow me" and "Come and see" to his disciples. I have often wondered how Jesus could be so brief with his two-word or three-word invitation, yet so effective. There was something so compelling about him, even when he said little.

Jesus' invitation rippled outward as Andrew invited Simon Peter, and before long Nathaniel asked a question of Philip, and over time, Simon Peter invited countless others to come and see the one they believed was the Messiah. When Andrew sought out his brother Simon Peter, he invited him after he'd spent only a short period of time with Jesus. It was a simple invitation but one that changed the world.

Now, why do we need to practise the question? We practise the question because we are out of the habit of asking the question, and to get into the new habit we practise it. The art of repetition is to go and ask the question, then ask the question again, then ask the question again! By repetition we will get better at it and acquire the habit of invitation.

Step 8: Prayer

You might have been wondering when we'd get to this – a spiritual step!

Prayer in our worship often seems as if it is us doing all the talking and none of the listening. I get concerned too about praying without expectancy. As someone who prefers to be active, it often leaves me cold.

Prayer is an ongoing communication with God, one in which God prompts us, whispers to us, answers us. I believe God is passionately interested in our everyday lives.

When going through the previous steps, I have asked church leaders to model a vision of a doubled congregation. Now what if this doesn't work?! You have two options: you could look through the paper for church vacancies and move to another church, or you could pray about it. In fact, we could pray for our own courage to invite, we could pray for those we are inviting, we could pray for other congregational members and the people they are inviting. In fact, we could pray for other churches who are having an Invitation Sunday. This could really mobilize prayer in the congregation. It might be urgent prayer, desperate prayer, or confident prayer; either way, the answer to the prayer will be turning up on the doorstep of the church. There is no hiding from the answer to this particular prayer. For many people this is the first step in mission and also in hearing God's voice.

Now, if there is no other step done, I know there will be a lot of praying!

Step 9: Make the invitation

This is the step we sometimes forget. Some of us are good at talking a good game, but never quite get round to actually making things happen. Again, a reminder at this stage, that success is one person inviting one person. Whether the person accepts or not is God's part of the process, not ours.

Very often I hear people say that they actually plucked up the courage to invite someone. To pluck up the courage is an interesting term, one the dictionary describes as: "The state or quality of mind or spirit that enables one to face danger, fear, or vicissitudes with self-possession, confidence, and resolution; with bravery."[4] This is interesting because we often use the word "courage" in association with real danger, such as on the battlefield. To use it so freely about invitation indicates just how deep-seated is our fear of rejection.

One of the interesting aspects of invitation is that people who have just been invited themselves and have stayed don't have a problem with offering invitation. It is often just those of us who have been in church for years that have such fear of doing it.

The King James Version of the Bible says there is a time and place to do everything, including inviting: "To every thing there is a season, and a time to every purpose under the heaven: A time to be born, and a time to die; a time to plant, and a time to pluck up that which is planted" (Ecclesiastes 3:1–2).

Winston Churchill once said that "Success is moving from one failure to the next failure, without losing enthusiasm." I am certainly not wishing failure on you, but it is the fear of failure that sometimes stops us from making the invitation in the first place.

Until we are committed to an idea, there is the chance to draw back, but the moment we definitely commit, then we can see how God moves too.

Successful inviters develop the habit of taking action

now. They try a new idea five or ten times before making a decision about it. They don't expect to do it right the first time. It is like riding a bike. Successful inviters have their invitations rejected over and over again but they get back in the saddle after each time and have another go.

Some people plant in the spring and leave in early summer before harvest when it looks as if the weeds are winning, but if only they had persevered, they could have enjoyed the harvest.

We need to develop the resilience of the sower!

Resilience is the positive capacity of people to cope with stress and adversity. The negative response to the last invitation may have been taken as a personal rejection and has stopped us from trying again. Contrast this "giving up" attitude with the life of Jesus and the early church, where there appears to be a remarkable resilience to rejection and persecution. Many early Christians were beaten, imprisoned, tortured and put in stressful situations, yet still Christianity spread. What made the early church so resilient when the church today seems to become paralysed with fear after even mild disappointments? It is almost as if rejection and persecution led them to an even stronger faith. I have heard many Christians say that what we need is a bit of persecution to sort out the church. This comes from the belief that testing makes faith stronger.

In fact, Matthew 5:10 says, "Blessed are those who are persecuted because of righteousness, for theirs is the kingdom of heaven."

We could exchange the word "blessed" for "happy". Happy are those who are persecuted and rejected. Could we say that about the church of today?

Another word that comes alongside resilience is perseverance. Could we develop a steady determination to start continuous invitation, despite the obstacle of potential rejection?

But let's cut to the chase. How do you invite? First, mentally prepare yourself, pray about it, find your friend, then just come out with it and ask. "Will you come to church with me?" Practise the question beforehand, in front of the mirror, the dog, or anyone who will listen!

Once someone in your congregation has invited a friend, whatever the outcome, we need to affirm them. This will empower them to do it again. Too often we affirm people only when they bring someone. This sends out the wrong signal to the rest of the congregation and is responsible for slowing down and eventually stopping future invitation.

And it is not just about those odd special Sundays, but every Sunday (or Wednesday or Friday or whatever day of the week your church meets for worship). I've been told about someone who did invite a friend on the special Invitation Sunday; they said they couldn't come that week, but they could make the following Sunday. The inviter then said there was no point in coming! We have to make any and every Sunday an Invitation Sunday.

Step 10: Walk or drive with them to the church service

Steps 10, 11 and 12 of the twelve steps to becoming an inviting church take us into continuous invitation. I am not interested in drawing a big crowd on one Sunday. I want to see us adding people to church week on week.

So the idea behind Step 10 is that once our friend has said yes to the invitation, go to pick them up on the day, and either walk or drive with them to the act of worship. In a real extension of the meaning of church, church starts the moment they answer the door. Walking or driving with them is as much being church as is the act of worship.

Many of us have had the experience of inviting someone and we are there at the porch of the church, knowing they are just not going to come. Then we find out on Monday morning that apparently two of their toes dropped off late on Saturday night, but they have managed to superglue them back on again as if there had never been a problem. You praise God for this miracle as you see them walking away normally.

So to take away our fear of them not turning up at the church, we need to go and pick them up. But we do this because of more than a fear of them not turning up. The phrase "go the extra mile" finds its place literally within this step.

To go the extra mile is to make more effort than is expected of you. This might really put you out. You might have to get up earlier than usual. You might have to drive a long way to collect your friend, or walk a distance. It might upset your usual Sunday routine. *But you do it anyway.*

Step 11: Introduce them to your friends over food or coffee

When people come on their own to church, it takes the effort of the congregation to notice the stranger and then transform the stranger into a sister/brother. The advantage of a bring-a-friend Sunday is that it is easier to help someone to break into the life of the church family.

You know your friend best, and can think in advance who he or she might enjoy talking with. Friends within the congregation can play their part that day by helping your friend feel really welcome. Often through conversation, your friend is able to find out more about the church and can discover that there are other people who have the same passions or interests as they do, and still are part of the church. They can explore other people's views and compare and contrast them with their own. Also, if you introduce them to your friends at church, they may feel more confident returning to the act of worship when you are away, if they know somebody else in the congregation. We grow most in relationship with God through our relationships with other people.

Step 12: Assume they will come to your church again

This is where the old curse reasserts itself, the "if they wanted to come, they would come" lock. But the locking curse changes subtly to "if they wanted to come *again* they would come!"

In the first year of Back to Church Sunday somebody told

me afterwards quite indignantly that I hadn't told them that they could ask their friends for a second consecutive week!

So are we going to fight against this curse by inviting them again? "Shall we do this again next week?" "Why not come to my home for Sunday lunch after the church service has finished?" This is a real extension of the meaning of church.

Very often at this point we are happy to pass the responsibility of coming to church over to our friend, but it still takes a brave person to come into a church building on their own, even on a second visit. Now, of course, our friend may say no to our second invitation, but that is OK. At least we have asked.

I want to finish this chapter by offering a caveat to my twelve steps that reminds us that though these steps may be (and I hope are) a helpful tool, God will still intervene in any way He chooses. God works over and above any process!

If you wanted to begin the process of changing your church's culture of being uninviting, where would you begin? What do you think of these suggestions?

- Try to get people in the church talking about who invited them and the circumstances.

- Ask congregational members what stops people in the congregation inviting their friends, then turn what you hear into sermon headings in the weeks running up to a focused Invitation Sunday. For example: "How can we invite when we have no other friends than the ones in this congregation?"

- Set the date for a double-your-congregation day and go for it. Remember to affirm people who are inviting and remind them that the invitation is in the question, not in the response.

- Then follow the twelve steps. For video clips on the twelve steps, go to www.unlockingthegrowth.com/resources.

Questions to think about

- Who invited you?

- When was the last time you invited someone to church?

- What made the early church so resilient when the church today seems to become paralysed with fear after even mild disappointments?

- Who has God been preparing in your life?

- Has God connected his people through friendship?

Chapter 5

The Reasons Why People Don't Come Back a Second Time

Starting to unlock the growth contained within a church is a bit like playing a computer game. There is always another level, another lock to break down and then yet another level to reach. And if you don't take down the locks one by one, well, you never reach the top.

Here are a few of the reasons I have been given why people don't come back to church a second time:

1. "28 people invited guests. Most seemed to enjoy the experience and the welcome. Some were quite emotional. Will they continue to attend? *We will see.*"

The "we will see" curse emerges to replace the original curse hanging over the church called "if they wanted to come they would come". Now that they have been once, we once again expect them to make all the running and it's not our responsibility to follow up or chase them again. Is it?

2. "A family who have been meaning to come to church since moving to the area a year ago *finally made the effort*."

The underlying message of these words is a critical one; all the responsibility for this family getting into and remaining within the church seems to be with the family, not the inviter or the church.

3. "A couple said they stopped attending a church years ago, and came back because a neighbour invited them. They were pleased, and asked their neighbour *if they can come back*."

Here we have the classic lock of not asking the visitor to come along again. In this case the couple were forced to do the asking themselves.

4. "I *hope* they will all return this next week."

Here at least the speaker almost expresses some optimism, but I doubt there is going to be any action taken by the church leader or the congregational members, apart from "hoping"!

5. "Many baptism families came back."

This is, of course, good news, but begs the question: What took the church so long to invite them again? Will there be an effort on the church's part this time to invite them again and again? The "many" brings to mind the numbers of families who, over the past years, have had a service of baptism, yet have never received a follow-up visit or an invitation.

6. "No good news – though we knew the people who came, none of them have come back since!"

One of the biggest locks we have to get over as a church is the fixation on church being the act of worship on a Sunday morning, and the idea that people are required to come to us rather than us being responsible for invitation.

7. "We could not easily identify the people who came in response to invitations."

This is a very subtle lock. In fact, it leads me to think that the church was not expecting visitors in numbers and did not have a plan to follow them up. So they had no idea who the visitors were and no way of contacting them to invite them back again.

8. "Two ladies who came said they had very much enjoyed it, and would be coming again sometime."

I love the word "sometime". But what does it mean? It could actually mean next week, in five years' time or possibly never. Remember, in these responses the original question I posed was, "Do you have any good news stories?" Is "sometime" a good enough news story?

9. "Some of the 'Back to Churchers' said they enjoyed the service and promised to return."

This lock is very innovative! We have good news here that people promised to return and now we can sit back on our laurels and wait! While this sounds like good news, it is not a cast-iron certainty. Other invitational possibilities should be planned to reinforce people's desire to return.

10. "We are pleased that some of the 'returnees' were younger families rather than older folk."

The "invitation discrimination" here is very obvious, with a desire to attract predominantly young families. It has been called "vampire evangelism" – a desire only for fresh young blood!

Unfortunately, the truth is that, leaving aside an Invitation Sunday, there are plenty of first-time visitors per year for most churches, yet the Back to Church Sunday analysis shows that only 10 per cent of those invited on an Invitation Sunday become regular weekly attenders of the church to which they were invited. That means a massive 90 per cent of first-time visitors experience the act of worship, the sermon, and the welcome – and do not return.

The locks show us God's agenda for the church. I believe the reason why we don't do anything about the locks of retention is that we never *expect* people to stay. We are so experienced in our disappointment that we know most won't stay, and so we express no surprise when people don't return, or we show little expectation that they should come again.

We don't know that we don't know about how to add to the church, and so we passively accept the status quo.

I worked with a number of church leaders in the run-up to an Invitation Sunday to see if they might be able to double their congregations and try to retain more than the 10 per cent. As part of the process I asked the church leaders whether they might ask a "mystery worshipper" to visit their church, to give them some feedback on how welcoming they were. One very brave leader sent me the following words from a family who attended as mystery worshippers. Here are their observations:

- "What a beautiful church – it's a shame the service did not come up to the building's standards."

- "Nothing has changed – it's just like church when I used to go with my Gran."

- "The congregation don't like children – there were three little girls in church with their parents and it was obvious from the turning around and tutting that some of the congregation did not approve that they were there."

- "The Vicar blessed the new hymn-books and people around us were tutting and muttering disapproval at the new books."

- "The choir were so old, I thought they would need resuscitating. When they process into the church the way they look sets the tone – it's a church for old people."

- "I thought singing and music was to enhance the worship, but the music was slow. Did anyone know the hymns? It didn't sound as if they did. We ended up laughing at the music and singing!"

- "There is a children's area but it's for babies. There is nothing suitable for a wide age range of children like our son."

- "If I wanted some motivation to become an atheist, attending this church was it!"

For some who only come once, it might be that they have been approached to give money, which reinforces so many people's negative views of the church. Or someone with a clipboard reached them before the church leader and tried to sign them up for the church cleaning rota, or being chair of the "we desperately need money committee".

For others, it might be the complications of the Eucharist/Communion – not just whether they should go up, but how the system for getting to the Communion rail actually worked.

Sometimes they are spoken to just once. I have heard the following one-liners said by church congregations to first-time guests:

- "You'll be needing this" (the greeter hands over a book, and no other word is said during the visit).

- "Can you move? You're in my seat."

- "I haven't seen you in a long time!"

- "What are we going to do with her?" (greeters wondering where to seat the guest).

The problem is that we just don't know why people don't return because most of the time we don't dare ask them.

Questions to think about

* When you first came into a church setting, why did you stay?

* What stops people coming back a second time to your congregation?

* How might you put things in place to encourage people to come again?

These questions should help us to identify the locks and the solutions to the locks. You will find the answer to more people returning to church by listening to the answers to these questions. But we need more too.

You may have watched the TV show *Undercover Boss*. Each week the cameras follow around a corporate executive who goes "undercover" to participate in various jobs. They get a first-hand look at how their decisions impact the employees, their morale – and much more. Do you, as a church leader, need to go undercover, or could you encourage a mystery worshipper to visit your church? Then you may really experience what a visitor to your church sees. It may not be complimentary, but until you know, you won't be able to make the changes that may encourage people to come again.

Chapter 6

The Seven Phrases that Turn Away

At the heart of the Christian faith is the action of *metanoia*, which means to repent and change our minds. But *metanoia* should also manifest itself in what we do, the way we act. We should start to see a difference as well as think it.

When we want to make a change in church, we often have to start with the leadership or management meeting. Somebody once said that a meeting is "an event where minutes are taken and hours are wasted". Many of us will testify to the truth of that statement! Unfortunately, those who want to innovate or change their church to make it more welcoming or inviting have to face facts about it, and that means discussing the results with church leaders. This is what often happens when people are confronted with change. It is known as *the five stages of innovation* (as quoted by Bill Bryson):

1. People deny that the innovation is required.

2. People deny that the innovation is effective.

3. People deny that the innovation is important.

4. People deny that the innovation will justify the effort required to adopt it.

5. People accept and adopt the innovation, enjoy its benefits, attribute it to people other than the innovator, and deny the existence of stages 1 to 4.[1]

You may have to go through all these stages at your church meeting!

I want you to imagine now that the mystery worshipper exercise has been undertaken and has thrown up a proposal that the church should keep the back pew/row empty for first-time visitors. And yes, I have checked that you can be surgically removed from the back pew! You now have to take this through your management committee. Let's imagine for a moment what their responses might be:

At Number 7: "We've never done it that way before." (Mrs Smith has always sat on the back pew.)

Sometimes it is hard for people to admit they are wrong. These are the people who just refuse to admit they are wrong, even when they are. These people are the ones who have a preconceived notion of how something should be. They are similar to the people who refuse to change or won't accept an idea.

At Number 6: "We're not ready for that." (We are really not ready to tackle Mrs Smith.)

Some of us think we really need more training courses

before we can do any Christian work whatsoever. I know of a church that is a "training church". They have been trained on everything; they are the Christian equivalent of the SAS. Unfortunately they have never been deployed. Why? Because they have another training course next week and the week after that on another aspect of the Christian faith. I wonder whether, as the seventy-three disciples were sent by Jesus on mission, one of them said, "I'm not ready for that", and so Jesus only sent the seventy-two.

At Number 5: "We're doing OK without it." (Why upset Mrs Smith? We are seeing some first timers.)

Is this being spoken by someone who is seeing thousands of people on a regular basis being added to the church? I'm afraid I can't think of any church right now that can afford to allow this type of thought pattern to develop amongst its leadership and management group.

At Number 4: "We've tried it once before." (We tried it when Mrs Smith was on holiday and nobody sat there.)

Successful people develop the habit of taking action now. They try a new idea five or ten times before making a decision about it. Don't expect to do it right the first time. Successful people fail over and over again.

At Number 3: "It costs too much." (There will be tears and tantrums and possible legal action.)

We have an unbelievably generous Heavenly Father and yet, across the church, there is often a mentality which says we must hoard away and build up our reserves (for good stewardship purposes, of course), and so we can never afford to be generous. The church is keeping the little brown envelope industry in business. For those of you who don't know what a "brown envelope" is, every visiting speaker at a church is normally approached by someone bearing a small brown envelope. This is the "gift" for doing the preaching, matched with a phrase practised by every treasurer: "This is towards your expenses." Every preacher then knows that the "gift" will go nowhere near to meeting one's expenses! The small brown envelope has three important features. First of all, it is small, so this reduces the risk of any church official (especially those new to the job) being too enthusiastic with the gift. Secondly, it is brown; the advantage of this is that the recipient cannot see how generous you are being. Thirdly, you can seal it, which means the person will never open it in front of you. The recipient can only get a real feel of the generosity if they can feel the coins!

The early church was dominated by stories of excessive generosity, in which people were selling their houses and combining the proceeds and providing for the poor and widows. Now there are millions and millions of pounds and dollars sitting in the bank accounts of churches and church members because we no longer get our security from God but from bank accounts.

I went once to speak at a large, prosperous diocese and had a five-hour round journey. I asked, gently, whether it might be possible to claim some petrol expenses, as I was speaking at a conference for them. They said "No." Enough said!

"It costs too much" is one of the most damaging and debilitating of the locks at a church management level, and it is time we challenged the way we think about and use God's money. I am not calling for the irresponsible use of money but a realization that He provides on a daily basis and, like manna, money can stink if stuck in a bank account for too long!

At Number 2: "That's not our responsibility." (We need to pass this over to…)

One of the most iniquitous words in church vocabulary is the word "secular", which we use to divide very neatly those things which are "spiritual" and those things which are not. This can sometimes lead to us think that we are guardians only of the spiritual. Our responsibility is to make sure that the church building is well repaired and fit for purpose, that the actual act of worship takes place, and that we keep all church members happy by having the right hymns or songs each Sunday, and the right length and content of sermon. Isn't it? This is what I call "club Christianity", where Christianity is for members only. Your membership of the club means knowing where you sit and attending regularly.

At Number 1: "It just won't work." (We will go through the pain of moving Mrs Smith but she will be back within the month.)

Remember this story? Twelve spies went to spy in Canaan. Ten of them said, "The people are giants and strong, and the cities are fortified. It just won't work."

Ten spies saw what they believed. But the other two spies, Caleb and Joshua, also saw what they believed. The result of "It just won't work" was forty years in the wilderness.

Could we be in the wilderness of unbelief right now?

The other way to monitor your important management meetings is to appoint a "but" watcher. This person is officially responsible for pointing out every time somebody uses the word "but"!

The antidote to these seven locks is the following words:

At 7: "Behold, He is doing a new thing" (Isaiah 43:19) replaces "We have never done it that way before."

At 6: "We can do all things through Christ who strengthens us" (Philippians 4:13) replaces "We're not ready for that".

At 5: "We need to be about our Father's business" (Luke 2:49) replaces "We're doing OK without it".

At 4: "We will reap a harvest if we do not give up" (Galatians 6:9) replaces "We've tried it once before".

At 3: "Our needs are supplied by God according to the riches of His grace" (Philippians 4:19) replaces "It costs too much."

At 2: "We are God's ambassadors" (2 Corinthians 5:20) replaces "That's not our responsibility".

At 1: "We are more than conquerors through Christ" (Romans 8:37) replaces "It just won't work".

Are you willing to change? We shouldn't always believe everything we think. We need to question the way we think.

We need to become more of who we really are. We need to release the passion, creativity and imagination that have been placed within us by God.

Questions to think about

- Do you agree with the seven responses listed above?

- Which one is the biggest turn-off in your experience?

- How might you apply the antidotes to these phrases in your church?

Chapter 7

Turning Failure into a Friend

One of the most challenging parts of my work has been to discipline my own disappointment when I hear church leaders say why they are not going to participate in another Invitation Sunday. It has been my experience that most church leaders will give anything a try once, but if it doesn't work, then they discard it. I have sat in meetings where I have heard leaders, who were all excited and expectant in the first year of organizing an Invitation Sunday, feel a real sense of shame when it didn't live up to their expectations. You see, sometimes God allows us to fail in order to bring us into a closer relationship with Him, so that we can see things more clearly. But at times it is embarrassing to fail. We have a model of church leadership that does not really allow failure. A church leader's goal is the transformation of a community, but God's goal is the transformation of the church leader.

We all know the story of Peter stepping out of the boat to join Jesus walking on the water, but in our own personal lives we try to avoid any type of risk that might leave us publicly embarrassed and privately humiliated.

When Peter stepped out of that boat he took a risk. Matthew 14 says when he saw the wind, he began to be afraid. He began to sink. But the glorious thing about this story is that Peter actually walked on the water. He took a risk, eventually failed, but boy, did he learn something in the process!

If we are willing to try anything and to take risks, we will fail sometimes. It's just the way it is. One definition of life is opportunity mixed with difficulty.

So after hearing the litany of why such and such a person did not invite, and why such and such a person did not come when invited, and why they didn't stay, and why the church is now too tired to invite, and why we need to change the act of worship first before we try this again, and why church leaders and congregational members are not interested in being trained, and why nothing will ever change, we eventually get to unpick the locks that have emerged. This is a very painful process for everyone involved. It is often very difficult to challenge our church leaders, as we are used to them having the answers.

In the story of Peter getting out of the boat there are parallels for what happens when things go wrong with a church leader. The litany of negative thoughts they produce is just what they have heard themselves, in their heads. These thoughts are just like the wind that blew, causing Peter to become afraid.

What Peter experienced when he stepped out of that boat was fear, and then shame, before control. The passage says that when he saw the wind he was afraid. He then cried out in his fear and shame, and the only way to control the situation was to ask for help from Jesus. But many of us don't ask God for help; we try to control the situation ourselves.

The shame–fear–control cycle

Shame, fear and control work together to bring failure into our lives. *Shame* says, "I am bad. I am different from everyone else." *Fear* says, "I am afraid that if anybody finds out how bad I am, they will not accept/approve of/love me." *Control* says, "I have to control my environment and everyone in it so that no one discovers my defect." If control is threatened in any way, what results is a never-ending cycle of:

- *Shame:* Shame is a painful feeling from the consciousness of something dishonourable or unworthy. Shame becomes an attack on one's self, one's own identity.

- *Fear:* Whether the threat is real or imagined, fear locks us, stifles us, and makes us freeze. The anticipation of something fearful stops us from seeing and taking opportunities, and from becoming who God wants us to become. Fear causes us to feel unprotected, unsafe, insecure. It stems from shame, as we are fearful that our shame, our defectiveness, will be exposed.

- *Control:* Control creates a barrier between ourselves and others, as we try to control them and control ourselves so our shame will not be exposed. Control imprisons us. It promises to protect us from hurt or pain, yet it usually fails. (Control almost always stems from fear and shame.)[1]

There are two examples in the Back to Church Sunday experience. A congregational member invites somebody who says no. They are ashamed that they have nobody to bring, and they fear being the odd one out and being questioned about it by other members of the congregation, so they decide to control the situation by missing church that Sunday. I have found that the last Sunday in September in the UK has become very popular for a timeshare break, or getting your caravan out for the last time before autumn really hits!

Then there is the church leader who tries an Invitation Sunday and encourages the people to invite. On the Sunday itself not one of the congregation brings a friend. The church leader feels personally rejected and ashamed, and fears that if any of their church leader colleagues finds out, they might be exposed as being a poor leader. So they control the situation by coming up with a phrase such as "It doesn't work for us."

There is another example of the shame–fear–control cycle in the story of Goliath and King Saul's army. The giant Goliath froze an entire nation in fear. In their shame, the only way the army and King Saul could cope with the fear was to stay on their side of the battle lines. But once the shepherd boy David came along and sorted Goliath with a single stone, hundreds of formerly intimidated men eventually became David's mighty men.

It is often how we view the problem that becomes the

real problem. King Saul and his army couldn't see past the giant Goliath, but David could, and saw wealth, the King's daughter, freedom from future taxes, and confidence in God. This was, after all, a story not about David and Goliath, but about David and God.

What church leaders experience when they fail is exactly the same as Peter and the army of King Saul. Shame tells them, "I am so bad at leadership that I couldn't get anyone to invite a friend." Fear tells them, "I am afraid that if anyone finds out that it has worked somewhere else, I might not be accepted by my congregation." Control tells them, "I have to control my sphere of influence so no one can discover my defect."

Terry Robson, in his book *Failure Is an Option*, says, "failure is the enforced pause that opens you up to new options", and "what seems like failure is almost always a redirection pointing you to places you are meant to be."[2] Failure is a perspective, and one person's failure is another person's success.

It was Thomas Edison who said, "If I find 10,000 ways something won't work, I haven't failed. I am not discouraged, because every wrong attempt discarded is another step forward." Often one of the best ways to hear God's voice is in the midst of failure, if only we stop berating ourselves to listen for it.

So are you a church into running away from failure or are you into feedback? Golfers learn most when a ball goes out of bounds. Tennis players find the net a way to reassess how they are playing the game. Feedback is the rocket fuel that propels the acquisition of knowledge. In fact, closed doors are often incredible blessings. Yet we as a church are not into failure. We think we cannot be seen to fail, and so we stick with the usual practices that have got us into the present situation.

The word "airbrush" has recently been adopted into everyday language. The phrase "airbrushed out" is used to describe photos where a model's imperfections have been removed, or where their attributes have been enhanced. But airbrushing also happens in church circles.

The church has a tendency today to airbrush out any imperfections. There is no way the church authorities of today would commission the writing of the Psalms. There is too much honesty there: "Why have you forsaken me?" "Why have you let my enemies surround me?"

What if we chose to look at our failures and imperfections as an aid to hearing God's voice?

Shizuka Arakawa, one of the best Japanese ice-skaters ever, reckoned she had fallen down 20,000 times in practice. Why did she put up with that?

She put up with it because she did not see falling down as failure. She saw it as evidence that she was improving and took it as an opportunity to learn to develop and adapt. What a lot of the stories of the disciples in the gospels, and those involving some of the Old Testament characters like Abraham, Isaac, Jacob, Joseph, Moses, David, and countless others, have in common is making mistakes, failing and at times being completely stupid. Yet God seems to have used them anyway. This is so encouraging, because my own life has been full of mistakes!

What Arakawa's example ought to teach us is that anything worth doing well, is worth doing poorly the first time.

A second quality we need to learn is resilience. In Chapters 2 and 4, we looked at how, in the Parable of the Sower, the Sower kept on sowing. He kept on sowing despite knowing that some of the seed failed to reach the good soil.

So often, however, church leaders have self-limiting beliefs, because they have never dealt with the failure in their lives. One church leader from Argentina once heard me say some years ago, "I could never do that" and told me that I was suffering from inverse pride. When we deny what God has designed us to be, we lock down the growth in our lives. We need to have the same view of ourselves that God has of us.

Bishop Tom Wright says, "God has prepared His people for a fuller version of humanity than we can imagine."[3]

For most of us, the skill and practice of expecting God to move has been lost or corrupted by years of frustration, disappointment, lack of belief, low self-esteem, or the half-truths we have accepted as whole ones.

What if we realize that failure is often God's teaching tool and we start to ask Him what it is that we need to learn? Revd Norman Vincent Peale used to say: "When God wants to send you a gift He wraps it up in a problem. The bigger the gift that God wants to send you, the bigger the problem

He wraps it up in."[4]

Problems are a sign of life and activity, but we get concerned with the wrapping rather than the gift. We need to ask what we are meant to learn from this problem. If we don't recognize the solution in the problem, it keeps coming around again and again. (Or is that just my experience?) So we might as well learn the lesson the first time around.

If we look for ways to learn from our disappointments, we might be able to move towards lament in our relationship with God. Lament is also on the other side of failure.

Walter Bruggemann defines lament as "impatient insistent protest"[5] at your present situation. It is part of the extraordinary vocation of the people of God within the overall plan that God has. You might think we lament enough already, but actually today, while there is plenty of resignation, passivity, blind acceptance of one's present situation, and numbness in our church leadership, there is little lament.

To lament is to courageously approach the Lord and protest over one's life, the state of one's community, and the materialism which so inhibits spirituality. To lament is to get honest with God about the state of the ministry to which He has assigned us. But lamentation and tears can only come when we deal with failure honestly.

Pain is the signal to grow, not to suffer, and once we have learnt the lesson, it goes away.

Albert Einstein once said, "In the midst of difficulty lies opportunity." If only we can accept that God speaks more through failure than success and pay more attention to our failings, we will see an incredible change in our lives as God turns our weaknesses into opportunities, as He releases the chains that have bound us, as He continues to shape us into the men and women of God we were always meant to be.

If I could get to every church leader in this success-hungry world, my one message would be to turn failure into a friend. We need to discipline our disappointment. Christ saw the rich young ruler walk away, saw many disciples turn back after a particularly hard teaching, saw Judas betray him, and the other eleven disciples temporarily desert him in the garden of Gethsemane. Jesus himself had to face disappointment.

Peter Brain, Bishop of Armidale in New South Wales, reminded me that the other problem is that we find it difficult to distinguish between our goals and desires. A goal is what nobody else can block me from doing, whereas a desire is that which requires God's working and the co-operation of others.

So, the goal is to lead by example and teach people to invite (one person), since no one can block that, whereas our desire is that people do it, that people respond, and that they become part of the body of Christ. We should pray for our desires and work for our goals, whereas we typically reverse this – we work for our desires and pray for our goals, which in turn leads us to get disappointed and lazy, stopping us from doing what we ought to do.

It was Paul who said: "I planted the seed, Apollos watered it, but God made it grow" (1 Corinthians 3:6). We serve a missionary God who is at work in the world by the Holy Spirit.

Failure is inevitable, so why do we beat ourselves up about it? It is an everyday occurrence. Success and failure are part of the same process.

Yet libraries are full of books on success, whereas there are hardly any on failure. Here are my six lessons to learn from failure, and tips on how to handle it when it happens.

Six lessons in failure

1. Most failures are avoidable with the benefit of hindsight, and usually we can see the clues in advance.

2. Success and failure are subjective terms, but we get to define the term. We put a burden of perfection on ourselves that is not right.

3. Both success and failure are temporary.

4. Success and failure are opposite sides of the same coin. Our value as an individual does not change depending on the circumstances we face.

5. Every failure can be overcome.

6. Failure is not a dead end, it is merely a detour.

Nine principles for handling failure

1. When you fail, get help from your faith, family, and friends. Those who matter don't care about our failure.

Those who care about it don't matter.

2. Acknowledge and admit your failure (instead of blaming everybody else).

3. See the failure for what it is (we tend to exaggerate the negative).

4. Compare it to your own history. List all your failures, list all your successes, look for a pattern and see what you can learn – but take note of the fact that you do survive your failures.

5. Learn how to forgive: forgive those who messed with you, forgive those who did not show up, and forgive yourself. We can't go forward looking backwards.

6. Learn from it – get value and benefit from it. Otherwise, you are doomed to repeat the failure. Recast the word "failure" as "experience".

7. Find a coach or someone you respect. They will help you to look at yourself as God sees you, and can help you to change your focus/perspective.

8. Get up and get going.

9. Keep going once you get going.

You are not the only one to fail, and fail again. Vincent van Gogh sold just one painting during his lifetime, and yet now his paintings sell for millions of pounds.

In his formative years, Ludwig van Beethoven was incredibly awkward on the violin and was often so busy working on his own compositions that he neglected to practise. Despite his love of composing, his teachers felt he was hopeless at it and would never succeed. Beethoven kept plugging along, however, and composed some of the best-loved symphonies of all time – five of them when he was completely deaf.

In his first film, Harrison Ford was told by the movie execs that he simply didn't have what it takes to be a star. Today, with numerous hits under his belt, iconic portrayals of characters like Han Solo and Indiana Jones, and a career that stretches across decades, Ford has clearly demonstrated that he does, in fact, have what it takes.

While today Steven Spielberg's name is synonymous with big-budget movies, he was rejected from the University of Southern California School of Theater, Film and Television three times. He eventually attended school at another location, only to drop out to become a director before finishing. Thirty-five years after starting his degree, Spielberg returned to school in 2002 to finally complete his work and earn his BA.

St John of the Cross wrote of "the dark night of the soul",[6] saying that when it comes upon you, the first thing you do is everything you can to make it go away, but if you surrender to it, you gain a feeling of release, then a feeling of relief, and then a strange feeling that you don't want it to end too soon, so you can learn all the lessons the failure will bring.

There is no failure in falling down; the failure is only in not getting back up again. So don't waste a good failure, because imperfect practice makes perfect, and failure precedes success.

Questions to think about

* Is failure often God's teaching tool?

* Think of a time when you failed. How did it feel? What did you do about it? Did you learn anything?

* Have you battled with huge amounts of failure and finally triumphed, like the Japanese skater?

* What are you struggling with in this area of personal/ church failure at present?

Chapter 8

Back to What? Releasing Your Brakes

We are all looking for something more. That is obvious from the TV programmes that we watch, in our millions, each week. We are inundated with "extreme make-over" programmes, offering make-overs for our faces, our bodies, our wardrobes, and our homes. We are offered facelifts, Botox injections, and nose jobs. We want to feel better about ourselves and we keep looking for that ultimate make-over, which will transform us, body and soul. The world may not know what it is looking for, but it knows it is looking.

As a society we find ways to make a living but we don't know how to live. So even though millions of us don't go to church, all of us ponder the question that underpins our very sense of self: Is this all that life is meant to be?

Are we living a life of limitation?

All of us, consciously or unconsciously, come to a conclusion of sorts about who we are, what we can do, what our purpose is, and all this is usually reached without weighing up any real evidence or logic. We just believe what we believe because we believe it. Once we have made that decision, we defend it and cling to those beliefs. Far too many of us have accepted a limiting assumption about who we are, and what we are here for. We are all of us under-achievers. But we can't change what we aren't aware of.

R. Buckminster Fuller said, "Everyone is born a *genius*, but the process of living *de-geniuses* them."

Mark Twain said: "The only difference between a rut and grave is the length and the depth."

In the gospel story of a fisherman called Simon we find a vision of what God had in mind for His church. In the stories involving Simon, Christ's love, acceptance, approval and discipline are all on display: all of which help Simon transform himself into who he was truly meant to be – Simon Peter. There are many Simons inside and outside His church today who don't know that God loves them, accepts them, approves of them and will help and discipline them to become who He meant them to be. God has an assigned mission for each of us. The popularity of those extreme make-over programmes should give us a clue that we all feel a deep yearning for something more, a yearning which has its roots in a disconnection from our Maker.

At times I have to hire a car to travel to a seminar. When you get in an automatic car, you have to start the engine with the brake depressed – but you have to release the brakes in order to get the car moving in a forward direction. Many of us forget to do this in our everyday lives; we still leave our feet on the brake pedals of life.

From the moment Simon follows Jesus, he starts to find in Christ a relationship that brings about transformation. He sees Jesus feed the five thousand, sees a child raised from the dead, and sees Christ, Moses and Elijah transfigured. He sees Lazarus raised from the dead. He listens to parables and asks Christ to explain them. These moments of crisis and teaching provide breakthrough moments in Simon's thinking.

Simon was capable of making great statements such as: "You are the Messiah, the Son of the living God" (Matthew 16:16); "You have the words of eternal life" (John 6:68); "Lord, I am ready to go with you to prison and to death" (Luke 22:33). He also made some terrible statements, rooted in fear, such as "Never, Lord" (Matthew 16:22) when he tried to stop Jesus following God's plan. He is convinced that he will never disown Jesus but then, terribly, he goes on to do so. He falls asleep when Christ needs him the most in the Garden of Gethsemane. He cuts off the ear of the high priest's servant.

Despite Peter's failures, Jesus reinstates him and shows him the task for his life ahead. He will continue to be discipled through the power of the Holy Spirit.

The Acts of the Apostles show a transformed Simon Peter, a man who preaches and adds thousands to the church. He is described by the authorities as unschooled and ordinary, yet he commands a man to walk in the name of Christ, he addresses the authorities and, despite his lack of education, he speaks powerfully to an astonished ruling class.

He shows wisdom in looking into the hearts of Ananias and Sapphira and in a prophetic utterance of what God was about to do as they were struck dead, in a dramatic punishment that created fear of the Lord (Acts 5:1–11).

His shadow is enough to heal all, and the Holy Spirit is imparted as he lays hands on people. As he preaches in Samaria, thousands turn to Christ. He has a dramatic release from his prison cell.

Within this story of an unschooled, ordinary man is a parable of the transformational nature of how the church is meant to be. How can these acts of great wisdom and shame belong to the same man?

Many of those involved in church leadership show more of Simon than Simon Peter, and yet they have to disciple God's people. Even leaders go only as far as their own intimacy with God. They can display a lack of hunger to learn. Leaders in a rut often think or act like this:

1. "My congregation is the cause of my problems."
2. "If only the congregation would change, my life would be better."
3. Demand that the congregation changes.
4. Threaten the congregation about their need to change.
5. Reward the congregation if they change.
6. "If the congregation changes first, I'll change."
7. Vent their feelings about the congregation.
8. Two forms of giving up: (1) the leader who quits and leaves; (2) the leader who quits and stays – this is the most dangerous leader.

In order for society to change, there needs to be a drastic and far-reaching change in our ways of leadership. Are we today like the children of Israel, who for forty years were circling in the wilderness? Often I hear church leaders say that we are "holding our own" in the circumstances. Is that the most we should be hoping for?

Unfortunately, Christianity today seems to be more about knowing *about* God than knowing God. It doesn't really matter how much you know if you don't use it. It doesn't really matter if you have degrees if you don't apply what you have learned. Have we watered down our faith? A lack of vision of what church is and should be, means that we experience a church politics where everyone is looking inwards, spending most of their time thinking about problems related to money, buildings and services.

- The fixation on *money* is about keeping as much of it as possible.
- The fixation on *buildings* has become crippling and limiting amongst many church families.
- The fixation on *services* has become a comfort that at least we are doing something worthwhile.

We have become congregations of people who find it acceptable that we are asking for volunteers for jobs. Everybody has to be on one or two rotas or they aren't seen as full, committed members of the church.

But rotas are a distortion of what God meant the church to be. This might sound crazy because we all need rotas to get anything done, don't we? But rotas of volunteers have replaced the idea that people should be appointed and anointed for the task.

Dwight Smith, a US church leader, said: "With what percentage of your church doing nothing with their faith would you be satisfied?"[1] The potential that we have in our congregations is staggering. If that potential is not being realized, it is extremely sad. God has given us every gift we need to extend His kingdom. One of my favourite verses in the Bible is: "we are God's workmanship created in Christ Jesus to do good works, which God *prepared in advance for us to do*" (Ephesians 2:10). It is one of life's great joys to see someone blossoming into the person they were meant to be.

Train, equip, release

The equipping of the saints to maturity is what Jesus seemed to be doing with Simon Peter and the other disciples. But if we are to follow in their wake, it will take a huge shift in our thinking about being disciples. For so long, we have been a pastoral community, but this fulfils only part of the vision of extending the kingdom of God. This mindset is holding us back. We need to be transformed into a corporate covenant-keeping people. The pastoral model has been one that services the congregation. It makes sure that everybody is getting what they want, including their favourite way of worship. It looks after the sheep and forgets the missing one or two outside the sheep pen. The discipling model discovers the brilliance within each one of our congregation and challenges people when they fall short of what they might be.

Discipleship is a process, which is why it is so important that there are courses like Alpha, Christianity Explored, Credo, Cursillo and the Start Course to help us with the important early questions.

In Mark 8:22–26 Jesus performs a miracle to teach us about faith and unlocking the potential within us. He took a blind man outside the village. Mark tells us, "When he had spat on the man's eyes and put his hands on him, Jesus asked, 'Do you see anything?'"

The now partially sighted man said, "I see people; they look like trees walking around." Then Jesus put His hands on him again and the man's sight was completely restored.

Did Jesus fail in His first attempt to heal the blind man? Of course not. Jesus had the power to heal the man the first time. He chose to do it the way He did.

It's as if Jesus chose to heal him in stages, like medical healing today. By doing so, Jesus is teaching His disciples, including Simon Peter, about faith.

It is very significant that this miracle happens between two stories where the disciples were struggling to understand Jesus (Mark 8:14–21 and Mark 8:31–33).

After Jesus touched the blind man the first time, the man could see, but he couldn't see clearly. This is like the disciples who were growing in their understanding of who Jesus really is. They knew Jesus and wanted to follow Him, but they didn't fully realize what His mission was. Jesus was, in fact, unlocking the growth within them, but doing so was a gradual process, not an overnight change.

Today, sadly, it is often the case that when people have gained some spiritual insight – perhaps they've followed a basic course like Alpha and come to faith through it – we leave them alone. They've passed the test, they're in, and all their questions about faith are now sorted. Aren't they? The trouble with that approach is that they often stay frozen in their fledgling faith.

A rapidly growing new area of scientific research is the Human Genome Project, which was working to determine the sequence of chemical base pairs that make up DNA and mapping the approximately 20,000–25,000 genes of the human genome. The mapping of the genes started in 1989 and was finished in 2004.

The church needs its own Church Body Genome Project, a research project whose primary goal would be determining the passions and gifts of the church. We would map them, release them, and make them available for the extension of God's kingdom.

As a father of three wonderful children, I marvel at the very different children my wife and I have produced. Each one has different passions, skills, and gifts. It is amazing how much variety there is in one family, and so it is with the church family – a variety of gifts for extending the kingdom of God.

So how might we make our first moves from the pastoral model to the discipling model?

Here are four phrases to bring out who we are meant to be:

- Know me
- Focus me
- Care about me
- Inspire me.

To *know* me is to understand that we are all God's workmanship, fearfully and wonderfully made.

To *focus* me is to help me become who I am meant to be in Christ. As Jesus did with Simon, we need to put love and hate into the same sentence: "I love you, Simon, but get thee behind me, Satan!" This is the goal of discipleship: the full development of all of your potential.

To *care* about me is to love me as God loves me.

To *inspire* me is to cheer me on and encourage me when I am falling. This is what Jesus did with Simon.

Through invitation we can begin the process of forming disciples. But many of our churches are really only interested in getting people into the pew.

Today, are we like Lazarus, raised from the dead, only to be left in our grave-clothes? Much of what we hear today is aimed at helping us to cope with living in grave-clothing. Becoming who God meant us to be should really be one of the major focuses of the church. Invitation asks people to listen for the prompting of God and then to act in obedience.

But God also uses failure to mould us into the person we were designed to be, as we've explored earlier in this book. Out of failure, out of crisis, God is doing more behind our backs than in front of our faces. Simon is not alone in being transformed in this way:

- Joseph was sold into slavery – but God was doing more behind his back than in front of his face.

- David hid from Saul – but God was doing more behind his back than in front of his face.

- Moses killed an Egyptian – but God was doing more behind his back than in front of his face.

- The children of Israel were pursued by the Egyptian army – but God was doing more behind their backs than in front of their faces.

- The rich young ruler walked away from Jesus – but God was doing more behind his back than in front of his face.

- After difficult teaching, many disciples walked away from Jesus – but God was doing more behind their backs than in front of their faces.

- The disciples ran away when Jesus was arrested – but God was doing more behind their backs than in front of their faces.

- The early church was persecuted and fled – but God was doing more behind their backs than in front of their faces.

- Jesus was crucified – but God was doing more behind the disciples' backs than in front of their faces.

- We all experience the wait of Easter Saturday – but God is doing more behind our backs than in front of our faces.

God wants us to discover who we are really meant to be. In the Bible, he took Sarai and she became Sarah. He took Abram and he became Abraham. He took Saul and he became Paul.

I am not only who I currently am and you are not only who you currently are. Though I don't know you, I do know something about you – that you have greatness within you and that God has given you the ability to do things that you cannot yet imagine. Catherine of Siena said: "Be who God meant you to be and you will set the world on fire."

God has a specific destiny and purpose for each person. For example:

- Jacob's first name meant "the Supplanter". God changed his name to Israel, "one who prevails with God".
- Simon was like a reed – unstable – but he became Peter, which means "rock".
- God changed Abram's name (which meant "high father") to Abraham ("father of a multitude"), and his wife's name from Sarai ("my princess") to Sarah ("mother of nations").

God changed their names to let them know they were destined for a new mission in life.

The word "genius" comes from the word "genesis" – to be born, to come into being. "Genius" is the word for someone's hidden potential.

So what is stopping us?

It is easy to look at a fruit, but when it comes to problems in our relationship with God, we need to look at the roots. We need to look for the cause and not the pain. We are meant to be living abundantly with God. To be able to release what is uniquely you, there are often blockages we need to unlock: self-doubt, unworthiness, fear, conditioning from parents, society, and the media – all of which suppress our God-given potential. (Neuroscientists say that our belief system governs 95 per cent of our thoughts, actions and beliefs are genetic.) What we hear and see and experience in our early years is programmed into our nervous system, and becomes our operating system. We may present with symptoms of being unfulfilled, and we need to look for the cause.

Can you believe and still have issues to deal with? Simon said, "My Lord and my God", and then betrayed Jesus. It can be hard for people to confess wrong thinking or sin. After all, aren't we all Christians? But, like Simon, we can still think, say and do the wrong thing, and we need people around us who will disciple us.

Look for the pattern of locks in your life and ask God to reveal any locks preventing you becoming who you are meant to be.

One of the ways I have identified patterns in my own life is through silence. On my first visit to Toronto I spent four days in a silent convent. At first the silence was irritating and I sought out people I could talk to. Unfortunately everybody else actually wanted to practise silence! After thirty-six hours I began to appreciate the silence and found a clarity of inner thought and conversation, which was very meaningful. In fact, when I eventually went back home it was a shock to discover a very noisy household and a very noisy world. Yet most of us can't live without noise, as indeed I thought I couldn't. As soon as I wake up in the morning, on goes the radio and that sets the pattern for the rest of my day.

But now, whenever I want some direction in my life, I usually pop in the shower. Invariably I come out not only cleaner but in the quietness, or the "white noise" of the water running, I find I can better hear God's inner prompting.

Often this prompting shows me I need to make changes to the way I am thinking and acting. We all need to learn to self-correct. Self-correction is the ability to initiate change and evaluate the results. We need to do this because we are living far below the potential that God had in mind. Our inner voice often tells us who we cannot be and what we cannot do.

It starts when we get negative feedback and it's a bit like monitoring the symptoms of disease in the body. At a doctor's appointment, a patient will be asked for their symptoms, to help the doctor to diagnose the root cause of the problem. There could be a number of potential causes but by asking a series of questions, the doctor narrows it down until, thanks to their training, they find the cause and can advise on how to treat it.

Three tools

To be able to do this in our walk with God, we need three tools: a suspecting tool, a detecting tool, and a rescripting tool. The key question we need to ask before we start is: "Where are my thoughts taking me?"

We seem to live off our experiences but then fail to learn from them. Failure to learn from experience is linked to fear of thinking things through.

The suspecting tool

A very good first question is: "What would give me an indication that I might have some poor thinking impacting on my life?"

Perhaps we are not completely happy with the level of the results we are getting. We need to look for familiar patterns and behaviours that we don't like.

The detecting tool

Two good questions to ask: "Does this thinking promote a sense of hopelessness about the future?" and "Does this thinking lower my sense of worth or power in Christ?"

The rescripting tool

Capture your own story in writing. As you read it through, look for places where you "own" your story and look for victim statements, where you have written yourself out of the story. Do you tend to exaggerate disadvantages or inflate adversity? Do you play down advantages and benefits? Write the story again, claiming all of it as yours.

Begin putting together a team of supporters or enlist the help of a Spiritual Director.

Decide what habits you want to master and focus on these, setting the others aside. Expose yourself to these insights each and every day, throughout the day, for the next three months, and apply them to your life.

Finally, have a vision for your life and get excited about your future! The Acts of the Apostles isn't, after all, entitled "The Beliefs of the Apostles". Simon Peter was transformed from Simon. The price you pay for security in life is lack of freedom to be all that God made you to be. So aspire to continue with the acts of the apostles in your community. Remember, extraordinary Christians are ordinary Christians who discover that they have extraordinary capabilities.

Questions to think about

- In what ways might we be living a life of limitation?

- "With what percentage of your church doing nothing with their faith would you be satisfied?"

- In what ways might the four phrases contribute to discipleship at your church? Know me, focus me, care about me, inspire me.

- Are the Suspecting, Detecting and Rescripting tools useful in your life?

- Does God have a specific destiny and purpose for each person?

Chapter 9

The Ten Keys to Keeping

Is yours a church that is easy to join? There are three roads to mission before we begin to think about the ten keys to keeping. Let me explain these roads further.

The first is the Damascus Road. This is the road on which someone encounters Christ, often dramatically, and is gloriously convinced of the Christian faith.

The second road is the Desert Road. This is the road where you keep reading the Bible and somebody comes along and explains what you are reading, and suddenly the passage comes alive and everything begins to make sense.

The third road is the Emmaus Road. This is the road where you are asking questions about God, and a friend comes along and journeys with you for part of the journey and explains a little.

In the ten keys to keeping, the Emmaus Road is the model of mission we want to pursue. God will send us people throughout our lives and our hosting job is to journey alongside them and explain what we know.

Many people ask how we will really know if we are a welcoming church. The best way to measure this is by what proportion of your first-time visitors return, and if they start to bring their friends. This is keeping. The ten keys give us the tools to really improve our welcome and increase the chance of adding people to the church.

Key 1: God sent you His precious people

We've explored in detail in previous chapters how first-time visitors are treated when they are brave enough to come into our churches. Our response afterwards is often dismissive: "If they want to come again they'll come", or "We'll see if they come next week". Not surprisingly, currently 90 per cent of our first-time visitors never come back and we often have no idea why they don't return.

The goal in many of our churches is to get people to make a weekly two-hour commitment to come to a building on Sundays – a real exercise in what you might call "bums on seats".

But we need to realize that nothing is an accident and that the people turning up on our doorstep have been sent by God.

If you really believed that God had sent every person who came to your church door, how would you change what you do?

Realizing how much God loves every human being and what God did through Christ for mankind will help us recognize the preciousness of every single person.

Each time someone crosses the threshold of the church, it is a holy moment and we should recognize it as such. God has some purpose in bringing them to you.

In the past, God sent people to His church in great numbers, but now God is doing something different, and the people coming to our churches now are not coming in by accident.

We will never be able to exceed God's highest expectations! God wants you to play a part in adding to His church every single person who crosses the threshold of the church building. This is a mission that matters and we need to be laser focused on achieving it.

Key 2: Church leaders should spend more time with newcomers than regulars

A recent survey by the Church of England weddings project showed that married couples see the church leader as the church. This gives us an important clue to how people who aren't regular members of the congregation view the church.

This means that regular members have to allow the church leader to spend time with first timers straight after the act of worship, and not tie them up in detailed discussions over rotas. We also need to encourage our church leaders to visit newcomers in their own home after the service.

The only way to increase the value of a relationship is to put more time into it. The only way you can increase the health of a plant is by giving it water, sunshine and fertilizer. Without it, the plant will die. The value of anything is determined by how much of your time you are willing to trade for it.

Key 3: Manage the first impression

We need to work out what people expect from church today. You can find this out by asking people who have joined you recently, or are not worshipping with you yet.

It may sound like common sense, but unfortunately it isn't common practice yet. Not everyone wants to be treated the way that we want to be treated. Some people want to be over-welcomed while others want to be under-welcomed. But how do you know what is the best approach for each person? We need to be other-person focused – it takes time and effort.

We should ask ourselves this question: How do we make it easy for newcomers to access the church?

Go the extra mile with any newcomers, or at least show them to a seat!

We can divide the first impressions people get from church into four areas: greeted, directed, treated and seated. Our teams on the door need to be trained so they know what they need to do to manage those first impressions. This includes:

- *Greeted:* welcomed with a smile. This might seem simple, but we have all been in churches where this does not happen!

- *Directed:* simply and politely shown where they need to go. Think about when you go somewhere for the first time – especially if it's a crowded room. How helpful would it be if someone gave you a quick explanation of what can be found where, first?

- *Treated:* shown respect, and offered food or drink.

- *Seated:* led to a comfortable, easy-to-access seat.

Key 4: The power of *lagniappe* ("Wait, there's more!" or "There will be surprises!")

In New Orleans the dialect word *lagniappe* (pronounced "LAN-yap") means "a little something extra". There is an old custom among merchants in New Orleans of adding a small, trivial gift to an order – particularly for large purchases or repeat customers. The word *lagniappe* originally comes from the Quechua word *yapay* ("to give more"), which led to *yapa* ("gift"), and then to the American Spanish *la ñapa* ("the gift"). Although the term *lagniappe* is not used in, say, Paris, the underlying principle appears in many forms in many cultures – including the "baker's dozen" that was once the norm in the UK.

There's a subtle yet powerful psychological principle at work here: the amount or quality of something you actually receive is not as important as how it measures up to what you were anticipating.

For *lagniappe* to function most effectively, it should be unexpected. A wonderful example of this principle is when Jesus made breakfast on the beach for the disciples. The fish must have tasted even more superb because it was so unexpected and was prepared by someone who loved them.

On Christmas Day in my church our leader produced a birthday cake with candles, which we lit. After singing happy birthday to Jesus, we all ate the cake during the service. It was totally unexpected, and a totally great cake. The power of *lagniappe*!

You could establish a church *lagniappe* team (with a budget) who could use their creativity to create a sense of appreciation and delight and to demonstrate how much God loves each one of us. Psychologist William James said, "The deepest principle in human nature is to be appreciated."

Appreciation changes things. I have altered a Mother Teresa quote slightly: "Be kind and merciful. Let no one ever come to 'our church' without coming away a little happier."[1] People come alive when we acknowledge and appreciate them.

Who can you team up to produce something purposeful with permanence? Remember, what they produce has to be unexpected, and will be all the better for it.

The *lagniappe* team could have the following four words as its vision: Meet to Exceed, to Delight, to Amaze.

Here's an idea for starters. How about bringing in the top chef in your area and treating your whole church to a sumptuous meal? Now if this sounds completely ridiculous, perhaps it is because our minds are only focused on church as an act of worship.

Are you willing to become a remarkable church, where people can come and be loved and respected and surprised?

If you pour on appreciation, not only will your normal

congregation not want to miss coming, but neither will your first timers. They will come for a second and third time. If they come back to you over and over again, they develop the habit of coming. This sounds so unspiritual, but good habits are hard to develop yet easy to live with, while bad habits are easy to develop yet hard to live with.

The power of *lagniappe* is limited only by your own imagination.

Key 5: Practise "Would you mind filling in the card?"

It is a simple question but it does not get asked as often as it should in a church. There are steps to take before this question can be asked. First, we need to create a card; second, we need to place the cards within easy reach; and third, we need to find a system that works to ask the question and get newcomers to consider filling in the card.

The phrasing of the question has to allow the visitor to say no, without feeling embarrassed, and that this is absolutely OK.

Some people will ask why they need to fill in the card. We need to know the answer to that question. One answer might be that we like to keep people informed about some of the activities going on at church. Or our church leader always likes to know their name, address and phone number so that he/she can give them a call later in the week.

Key 6: Contact first timers within the first week, if not within the first thirty-six hours

A handwritten note shows that you have taken the time to appreciate your visitors.

An appreciation call simply thanks the visitors for their visit. It is just like a thank-you letter, using your voice instead of a pen and paper.

Think about how you would do this if you doubled your congregation in a day. What if you had a large baptism party – how would you manage it then? Think it through and have a plan in place.

Key 7: Go and visit first timers in their homes

Call and ask if you can visit. A face-to-face visit allows you to listen "between the lines" of what people are saying, and you may be able to help uncover God's call in their lives.

Key 8: Send three invitations asking people to do something fun with the church

Invite them to dinner, a film night, a quiz night, a walk, or whatever else you can think of!

Key 9: Introduce them to a small group

Our commitment to one another, forming deep relationships, is so important to God. Close friendships and small groups are important, as it is in small groups that close relationships can develop.

In the early churches, pictured vividly by Paul in Romans 16, fellowship was often over a meal. There are few things more effective for building fellowship than sharing meals. It is perhaps partly due to this that the early church grew so fast, even in times of persecution. This combination of food plus small groups has been part of the huge success of the Alpha course today.

Time-of-life groups are wonderful for nurturing a relationship with God. They provide fellowship and companionship. They include:

• Youth Group

• Young Adults

• Engaged Couples

• Young Married Couples (or Double Income No Kids)

• Full Nest

• Empty Nest

During the Wesleyan revival John Wesley encouraged single-sex Bible classes which helped people to share:

• what sins they had committed

- what temptations they were facing

- what means of grace God was opening up (Scriptures, fellowship, opportunity).

Key 10: Transform your welcome team into a keeping team

It is time to establish a new ministry in the church. It is almost certainly in existence in individual members of your congregation already, but it has gone unaffirmed and unnoticed. It is the ministry of connection. We need to institute this ministry and set people free into it. Our church has to offer world-class hospitality and ensure that every new person or family has a companion to help them along their own Emmaus Road. Are you a church where people can make friends? In my church, I believe that our keeping team are going to make sure that the first-time visitor breaks into the life of the congregation. When my family and I moved to a new area, we went to check out the churches in the location. We only visited one, because of Margaret Bennett. Margaret made it her job to make sure that my family and I were introduced to people in the congregation. As newcomers, Margaret made us first her friends and always kept an eye out for us to make sure that we were having conversations with people right across the congregation. She had a pastoral ministry of keeping.

The ministry of connection tries to establish the church as a place where (to borrow a phrase from the eighties TV comedy *Cheers*) "everyone knows your name".

Before and after every service, have a short meeting to work out how you could have done better in hosting and welcoming.

Cross-congregational hosting

Underlying the ten keys to keeping is the concept of cross-congregational hosting, where everybody in the congregation is empowered to host. *Can you become a church where hosting is an act of worship?*

We need members of our congregations to behave like owners and hosts, not guests.

They should not just act like the host but be the host. Just as Jesus took up the basin and the towel, we must also get our hands wet (and dirty!).

Whoever sits near a first-time visitor needs to own the opportunity to be the host for that visitor. But to do this we need to think about how we already treat regular members of our congregation. Do they feel loved and welcomed? Human beings with heart and soul are the messengers of God. We need to concentrate on the quality we offer within the four walls of our church building. Our personal interactions with one another are moments of truth.

But sadly, instead of focusing on this, most churches concentrate on keeping the operation going. You can see this on a Sunday morning as the active members of the church are busy at various tasks to prepare for the act of worship. It is often in our busyness that we miss the opportunity to host.

When I hear the stories of people who stay after the first visit, they often tell me of someone in that congregation who took the time to connect with them. *The truth is that at any given time, one person in the congregation represents the entire church.*

We are the thirty-second commercial for our church. *The best way of unlocking the growth in your church is by word of mouth. What is the word on your mouth about your own church?* Empowered hosts will result in people being added to your church. But wonderful hosting will lead to many people crossing the threshold of your church building. If you take good care of your first-time visitors, they will open doors you could never open by yourself.

So how do you go about forming a relationship with someone you don't really know? We need to remember the one true secret of good hosting and act accordingly: you will be judged by what you do, not what you say. How can our congregational members add their personal signature to the way they host? Who can I make feel good today?

Give something back to your community and take the hosting concept out locally. And while we are at it, *what is the word on the streets of your community about your church?* Are there people of goodwill in your community who will recommend you to others without being asked? I don't mean people in your church congregation already, but those who don't yet attend. Are we creating relationships where people have high regard for you and/or what you stand for? Who are your community advocates, your key influencers in your community? It is not about people being willing to put in "a good word" for you when you ask them; it's about them doing it without being asked.

If you are a church leader, consider spending as much time each week on embedding the concept of hosting in your congregation as you do on actually planning the act of worship. Over-emphasis on the act of worship works to the detriment of simple mission.

Make sure a hosting culture is modelled in your church leadership:

1. Give authority to the congregation to host.

2. Preach and encourage individual initiative.

3. Encourage the concept of *lagniappe*.

Are we sure of what are trying to achieve? We are trying to see if we can turn ordinary congregation members into extraordinary hosts, to make sure people who cross the threshold of your church building feel as if they are the most important person in the world. Christ demonstrated how important each one of us is to God, and we need to demonstrate that too.

Questions to think about

- Is yours a church that is easy to join? What proportion of first time visitors do you keep?

- Which road to mission is your story based on – Damascus, Desert, Emmaus or another?

- If you really believed that God had sent every person who came to your church door how would you change what you do?

- How might we use the power of *lagniappe*? Can you become a church where hosting is an act of worship?

- What is said on the streets of your community about your church? Are there people of goodwill in your community who will recommend you to others without being asked?

Conclusion
Igniting Spontaneous Invitation and Not Being Able to Stop It

We all have parents, older relatives, brothers and sisters, sons and daughters, nieces and nephews that we pray for in the hope that one day they might come back to God. They may have left their childhood faith behind, dropped it by the wayside, but we pray that one day they will respond to the call to come back. Sometimes the very fact of our close relationship with them gets in the way of them listening to us talking about God.

But we mustn't forget that just because we seem unable to, it doesn't mean others can't reach out to our family. In fact, if you have a teenager you can tell for a fact from the phone bill that though your son or daughter doesn't want to talk to you, they are willing to hold in-depth conversations with others! In our turn, we can reach out to other people's families. A bishop once told me that his brother, who had not been to church in years, was invited to go by the principal of the school where he was teaching, and he has not stopped going since! He had prayed for his brother for years, and so was delighted, even though he personally hadn't been able to reach him.

Can we ignite spontaneous invitation in such a way that it is impossible to stop? Can we imagine people actually spontaneously inviting on any and every ordinary Sunday, rather than having to wait for a special Sunday?

What is stopping invitation?

We have already looked at the idea that culture eats strategy for breakfast. But there is not only a congregational culture, but also a church leadership culture to bring into the light and examine. I have found that most church leaders are happy to try an initiative once, so they can rule it out! So in early 2011 I conducted some research with some of those in our churches responsible for mission and for communication at seven regional meetings. At each one, I was given a series of reasons why churches are reluctant to invite:

- "I can't come that Sunday," said the person being invited… OK – I'll ask again next year!

- What if we end up giving two invitations to the same person? Some other church might have invited them!

I then asked why congregations don't invite again, after they have tried it once or twice. Here are the responses I received:

- We tried it and it didn't work.

- Why would you want to invite someone to this? (Feelings of shame about our acts of worship.)

- Too close to harvest. / It's at the wrong time of year.

- Initiative overload –there are just too many programmes going on to take on another one.

- People came but didn't stay. (Disappointment.)

- The Bishops are against it/senior leadership are not backing it because they didn't think of it.

- No one to invite./No friends outside of church.

- Club church – all the activities are based on keeping the present congregation happy.

- Nobody was invited.

- Large churches are already comfortable.

- It won't work.

- Leaders don't get their act together in time/no preparation.

- Leaders would rather not fail.

- The English psyche: we don't talk about religious affiliation.

- Little sense of why I come.

- Success is keeping the show on the road and survival is a measure of that success.

- We are a growing church and do this every Sunday.

- I tried inviting but they didn't come.

- I put a whole pack of invitations at the back of the church.

- General mission weariness.

- Guilt – to mention a mission of invitation brings us face to face with our own omission in this area, which can be uncomfortable.

- Maintenance sucks up energy.

- Some smaller churches need to die.

- Church is too far off the mark –we are just not relevant in our society, so why invite?

- Lack of confidence in God.

- Unrealistic expectations.

- Church leaders don't like to be told what to do – any instruction coming from the hierarchy above is seen as interference.

- I don't like ordering the resources on the website – because the administration systems are seen as complex, we won't be holding an invitation Sunday.

- My parish/church share will go up – more people means a greater financial contribution that churches need to find to pay out to their denomination.

- Is this the right Sunday to invite people?

- How do we keep the momentum going? We've done this five times already.

- When inviting someone to your church there is a sense of risk and you cease to be in control.

- We have never been asked to invite.

- No local champion at congregation level.

- Problems with getting ministers enthusiastic.

These answers reveal the culture that a leader has to tackle but also their own leadership culture. There seem to be considerable locks to overcome in this long list before we can ignite spontaneous invitation. But most of them could actually fit under only three headings, which are:

1. It didn't work.

2. Congregations not confident about inviting people to their acts of worship.

3. It's too close to Harvest./It's at the wrong time of year.

1. It didn't work

This crops up in various guises, including:

(a) We leafleted the whole area.

(b) Nobody invited anyone.

(c) The congregation invited but their guests said no.

(d) The guests came but did not come back a second week.

This is the most powerful reason locking spontaneous invitation. But how many things did Jesus do that, humanly speaking, didn't work? What about the rich young ruler turning away, or Judas betraying Jesus, or the disciples running away, or Peter denying Him, or the fact that He failed at times to get His message across to the disciples? Did it always work for Jesus?

(a) We leafleted the whole area

The constant barrage of leaflets through the door is part of modern life. We put up with the intrusion but we all know that most of our junk mail goes straight in the bin. The barrage of leaflets must work for the businesses who do it, or else they wouldn't bother, but the returns are very low. And as churches we have be aware that everyone wants to feel special. In fact, everybody is special, for as the Psalmist says, we are fearfully and wonderfully made (Psalm 139:14). Bulk mailing diverts us from the path of reminding people that they are loved and created by God.

(b) Nobody invited anyone

It looks like failure, but actually it's real breakthrough to know that your congregation has a problem with inviting family and friends. Has God given you the area to explore in teaching and discipling with people?

(c) The congregation invited but their guests said no

Isn't this success, in a way? The congregation invited and had a response from their guests. Success is one person inviting one person. Sometimes we will never know what God is doing in someone's life. The very fact that his church touched that person through invitation is incredibly profound. Jesus taught us that the success of the Sower was that he kept on sowing. We need to keep on inviting.

(d) The guests came but did not come back a second time

We need to ask questions to discover if they were invited again. Or did we leave it to our guests to come themselves? But even if they only came once, they still heard the Bible, participated in an act of worship, and the church may have touched their lives in some way. We may never know what God will do with an invitation, in the long term.

In today's success-hungry church we would probably rewrite the mission of the seventy-two disciples sent out by Jesus, and question whether they had any success at all. Remember that Jesus anticipated that they would have to wipe the dust from their feet and that people would not welcome them (Luke 10:11).

In the success-hungry church, "It didn't work" is the prevalent pathetic thinking that abounds. Let's compare the thinking of the church today with that of the church of the first century:

- On the Day of Pentecost some made fun of them ("It just isn't working"). Then Peter stood up!

- Peter and John were seized by the authorities and jailed ("It just isn't working"). Then Peter was filled with the Holy Spirit and courage.

- Then the apostles were jailed by the jealous Sadducees ("It just isn't working"), but when they were released they continued to tell the good news.

- The apostles were flogged ("It just isn't working"), but rejoiced "because they had been counted worthy of suffering disgrace for the Name" (Acts 5:41).

- Stephen was seized and brought before a court ("It just isn't working"). He was stoned to death, and they laid their coats at the feet of Saul.

- Persecution ensued. Good men were dragged off to prison ("It just isn't working"), but they were scattered as far as Phoenicia, Cyprus and Antioch, taking the good news wherever they went.

- Saul breathed out murderous threats against the Lord's disciples ("It just isn't working"), but on the road to Damascus he encountered the risen Jesus and was converted.

- Saul preached in the synagogues with power, but the authorities plotted to kill him ("It just isn't working"). However, a basket was provided to lower him to safety.

- Then they enjoyed a time of peace.

- After a while King Herod had James the brother of John put to death, and he also put Peter in prison ("It just isn't working"). But an angel released the chains and Herod was struck down and the word of God continued to spread.

- In Antioch Paul and Barnabas preached the word of God powerfully, but the leading citizens stirred up persecution against them and expelled them from the region ("It just isn't working"). Yet the word of God spread throughout the region.

- At Iconium Paul and Barnabas discovered a plot to stone them and they fled to Lystra ("It just isn't working"), but a great number of Jews and Greeks in Iconium believed.

- In Lystra the plot to stone Paul was executed by citizens of Iconium who had followed them, and Paul was left for dead ("It just isn't working"). But many believed and Paul was rescued alive.

- There was a disagreement between Paul and Barnabas over John Mark ("It just isn't working"), but two went to Cyprus and two more went to Syria and Cilicia, where the message was preached.

- Paul and Silas were arrested, imprisoned, flogged, and had their feet fastened in stocks ("It just isn't working"). But they sang praises, and an earthquake ensued, opening the prison doors and releasing them from their chains. The jailer was converted to Christ.

- The Jews were jealous, so they started a riot in Thessalonica, dragging the believers before the city officials ("It just isn't working"). But the believers sent Paul and Silas to Berea, where many believed.

- The Jews from Thessalonica came and caused trouble in

Berea ("It just isn't working"), so Paul went to Athens, where some sneered and others became followers.

- In Corinth the Jews became abusive towards Paul ("It just isn't working"), so he went to the Gentiles and many of them believed.

- Compelled by the Holy Spirit, Paul headed towards Jerusalem. Wherever he went, he was warned by the Holy Spirit that he would face hardship and prison ("It just isn't working"). But Paul was able to report to the Jerusalem Council about the thousands of new Gentile believers.

- Paul was saved from the mob and arrested in Jerusalem by Roman soldiers ("It just isn't working"). He spoke to a massive crowd who rejected him, but as he was about to be flogged by the soldiers, Paul said he was a Roman citizen and they stopped the flogging. He went on to testify to the Sanhedrin.

- Paul was saved from a plot to kill him and was transferred to Caesarea, where eventually he testified before Felix. He left Paul in prison for two years ("It just isn't working"). But Paul was eventually brought before Felix's successor, Festus, and King Agrippa, to whom he also testified ("It just isn't working"). But he appealed to Caesar and was sent to Rome.

- Paul was shipwrecked and the ship was broken in pieces ("It just isn't working"). But the Roman centurion wanted to spare Paul's life.

- Paul was bitten by a snake in Malta ("It just isn't working"), but he went on to pray for the chief official's father, who was healed.

- Paul eventually reached Rome and was kept under guard for two whole years ("It just isn't working"). During this time he was able to greet and preach to people.

The curse of success over today's church is summarized by "It just isn't working." Where is the backbone of the church today? We need to remember that God has ordained seasons of life. Wintertime can bring disappointments, and disappointment is common to all of us. So we must learn how to handle the winter season of our lives. We must learn how to handle adversity; it always comes after the opportunity of springtime. Dr Denis Waitley says: "Failure is the fertilizer for success."[1] The author and speaker Jim Rohn writes:

> *The big question is, What do you do about winters?*
> *You can't get rid of January simply by tearing it off*
> *the calendar. But here is what you can do: You can get*
> *stronger; you can get wiser; and you can get better.*
> *Remember that trio of words: stronger, wiser, better. The*
> *winters won't change, but you can.*[2]

2. Congregations not confident about inviting people to their acts of worship

As a church we have lost confidence in what it is we do. This is mainly because of our acts of worship. We have convinced ourselves that we need to be much better than we are at the moment. We sometimes believe that church is *only* the act of worship. So we think:

(a) Why would we want to invite our friends to this?

After all, the reason many of us go regularly to church is because we feel a sense of duty. It is an act of worship to God, but many of us are actually looking for the act of worship to do something for us. We want to be entertained because, after all, there are so many other things we could have done on a Sunday morning, aren't there? But surely this is the wrong question. The question should be, how might we offer acceptable worship to God? Is this about us or about God?

Or we tell ourselves:

(b) My friend just wouldn't be interested

We do a lot of thinking for our friends, and we make assumptions about them which stop us inviting them in the first place. These assumptions may have a hint of truth about them but they may also be wrong, which is why we need to keep inviting. In our rational, enlightened world where we value good thinking and judgment, I was always taught that to assume anything makes an "ass of u and me".

3. It's too close to Harvest / It's at the wrong time of year

We are a busy church, keeping the show on the road, what with our festivals and other special Sundays. Invitation would be much better if it happened at another, unspecified time in the year when we're not quite so busy, thank you very much.

What is more important – an act of worship or invitational mission? Should invitation be confined to only a couple of special Sundays? What does God tell us about this?

A trapped church

These are the three main reasons why we cannot ignite spontaneous invitation. However, as we examine these reasons, we can see they don't really hold much water. And underneath these reasons we have a church that is trapped either by the regret of the past or by the routine of the present.

The routine of the present

"You can have fifteen minutes." The number of times I have heard, "We can just about squeeze in a mission item, but you will need to be quick," is very painful. The agendas of churches in the West are packed and arranged sometimes many months in advance. If John Wesley had a new idea today, would he be given only twenty minutes to share it before his time was up?

The regret of the past

Being a generation of church leaders who have not seen exponential growth, there is an unspoken but enduring memory of disappointment and discouragement. We are carrying so much regret. Many entered the ministry with the idea that all we had to do was preach, and they would come! Disappointments are unavoidable but being discouraged is actually a choice. Discouragement often becomes indifference; we just don't care about those who are not with us yet. Many church leaders are just keeping their congregations happy and are stuck in a rut. How can we as present church leaders get over the regret? Answer: we need to stop running our own lives and hand them over to God. For it is God who gives the growth.

It takes consistent self-discipline to conquer the nagging voice in our minds, the fear of failure, and the curse of indifference. It takes discipline to change these poor habits. For every disciplined effort there is a multiple reward. If you tackle the fear of failure, the regret of the past, and the curse of indifference, you will see incredible fruit in your life. Present-day reality is always the best beginning. If we can bring ourselves to state the truth about the situation, the Bible says the truth will set us free. The problem is that human beings have an incredible ability to stare truth in the face and not see a thing!

Becoming who God meant you to be as a leader

God has not finished with you as a leader. God still wants you to become more of who He meant you to be. It takes time to build a congregation of disciples, it takes time to make changes in habit and discipline. So have patience. But be persistent, and tenacious. Impatience labels disappointment as failure. Don't let the small things discourage you. Persistence is patience in action. We need to be resilient and have the ability to withstand setbacks, for there will always be some in our lives.

Here are some ideas that may help you to move in the direction of spontaneous invitation.

The six laws of God which will ignite spontaneous invitation

I often hear the complaint, "I don't have enough time." I suspect that if we did a time-and-motion study on most church leaders, we might find that we are working on low-priority stuff. Parkinson's law impacts us all as church leaders. That law says work expands to fill the time allotted for it. The fact is, we have all the time there is. God gives us twenty-four fresh hours every day. The most significant work we can do as extraordinary church leaders is thinking and praying. Thinking and praying about what we do first, what we do second, and what we do not at all.

1. The law of posteriority

So in order to find time, we need to learn the law of posteriority.[3] We know about priorities, but what is posteriority? Posteriority, if you remember, is those things we need to do less of, do later or not do at all. We will never catch up with all the things we need to do. Therefore we need to set priorities and understand posteriorities. This can be urgent stuff, such as a ringing telephone or an email, but it is not the most important thing. A great insight for every church leader is: You can control what you do first, what you do second, *and* what you do not at all. When Andrew spent some time with Jesus, the first thing that he did was to go and find his brother (John 1:41). He could have gone fishing to earn money, but that was not his priority. When the apostles were approached by the hungry widows in the early church, they said it was not right for the apostles to serve on tables, so they appointed seven good men, while they concentrated on the ministry of the word of God (Acts 6:2). How are you being deflected from that which is God's priority for your life? Are you majoring in the minor things?

2. The law of correspondence

Secondly, we need to rediscover who God thinks we are in the law of correspondence, which can be summed up as follows: "It's not what happens to you that determines your happiness. It's how you think about what happens to you."[4]

The law of correspondence helps us to unleash our unlimited potential. For example, when you look at, say, a relationship or a church that seems as if it is struggling, one person will say, "This thing is struggling – I wonder how long we can hang on", while another person says, "It's not doing as well as we'd like. What can we do to make this work?" And these two approaches will lead to two completely different results! And so the lesson here is, check your viewpoint.

The law of correspondence is a mirror. The only thing you have to change is your thoughts. If you are consciously walking around telling yourself that your life is miserable and that you're just not smart enough or good enough, you will create misery and an environment where you feel inferior. This law says, "As it is on the inside, so shall it be on the outside." It can be summarized in these words from the Lord's Prayer: "Thy kingdom come, thy will be done, on earth as it is in heaven."

Here is a daily exercise for all of us. Repeat these phrases to yourself and act accordingly:

Telling the truth in advance

- In Christ I am God's ambassador.
- In Christ I bear much fruit and my fruit remains.
- In Christ I am God's friend.
- In Christ I am chosen and appointed by God.
- In Christ I am being transformed by the renewing of my mind.
- In Christ I am blessed with every spiritual blessing.
- In Christ I was chosen before the foundation of the world.
- In Christ I am loved with God's great love.
- In Christ I am His workmanship created for good works.
- In Christ I have access to the Father through the Spirit.

Just living one of these affirmations will transform your life! But, as the essayist G. K. Chesterton said: "The Christian ideal has not been tried and found wanting. It has been found difficult and left untried."[5]

3. The law of reversibility

This links closely with the law of correspondence. The law of reversibility says that feelings and actions interact on each other.[6] If you feel a certain way, you will act in a manner consistent with that feeling. However, the reverse is also true. This is a very powerful law for all church leaders and congregational members who are seeking a deeper walk with God. Even if you don't feel a certain way in your Christian life, if you act as if you do, the actions themselves will trigger thoughts and emotions consistent with the actions. We need to get our thoughts and feelings in line with what God thinks. Once you know who you are in Christ, then you will start acting in line with that knowledge.

A daily question for us all: How would the person God has made me to be do the things I am about to do?

4. The law of belief

This law states that we do not believe what we see; rather, we see what we have already decided to believe.[7] The more intensely we believe something to be true, the more likely it is that it will be true for us. Many beliefs have been handed down from one generation to the next and we have swallowed them without testing them. We should challenge our beliefs. Are they serving us? Do you really believe that nothing is impossible with God, or have you decided to believe something different? If so, write down that belief and examine it in the light of church tradition and Scripture. One of the beliefs that is prevalent in the church today is, "I'll believe it when I see it" – which is why our ministries are not effective!

5. The law of expectations

This law says that to believe is to assert in your mind the hope that what you have asked for can be manifest.[8] But to expect is to know without doubt that you will receive. Let me say this: Prayer can be a complete waste of time if you pray but don't *expect* that what you are asking for will be made manifest. Expectations are ideas that are built on solid rock. They are unshakable – unlike hopes and wishes, that will wash away with the first storm that comes along.

Your results are the outcomes of your expectations. For most of us the skill and practice of expectation has either been lost or corrupted by years of frustration, disappointment, lack of belief, low self-esteem, or half-truths that we've accepted as whole ones. We need to move from positive thinking to positive knowing.

6. The law of attention

Psychologists have discovered that the very act of observing a behaviour tends to change that behaviour for the better.[9] This

173

is one of the greatest breakthroughs in the understanding of personal performance. When you observe yourself engaging in any activity, you become more conscious and aware of that activity, and you do it better. For example, the activity of mobilizing invitation needs to be given serious attention in our generation. It was said of Charles Dickens that he did each thing as if he did nothing else. We need focused concentration, going around the obstacles of negativity. This takes a lot of discipline.

Once we get into the law of attention, we can develop some expertise in the area of invitation. Below are some more principles that will help us do that.

The Minutes Principle for individuals

Estimate how many minutes per week you spend face-to-face with non-Christians. This is your baseline. Now determine to double the number of minutes you are going to spend with non-Christians.

Who we invite depends on the amount of time we spend face-to-face with non-Christian friends. Who does God want me to spend more time with? Ask these friends for a coffee, a dinner or a walk. You can only increase the value of a relationship by putting more time into it, just like you help a plant to grow by spending time with it, watering it, allowing the sun to shine on it, and adding fertilizer.

Remember the law of sowing and reaping: In order to reap a harvest we need to plant in the spring. As we sow in our friendships, so shall we reap.

The Minutes Principle for churches

Estimate how many minutes per week Christians spend with non-Christians. Now you have your baseline. We are going to double the number of minutes we spend with non-Christians. This is a whole church activity where together we give attention to spending time with those outside the four walls of our church buildings. Church leaders can help their church members by having a lot of activity in the church building to which non-church members can be invited, such as:

- Mother and toddler group
- Who Let the Dads Out? (www.wholetthedadsout.org)
- Coffee morning/afternoon tea
- Curry and quiz night
- Book reading club
- Dance class
- Talent competition
- School choir and music festival
- A night at the movies with popcorn!

These are just a few ideas. A quick search of your local newspaper will throw up many other creative ideas.

Ninety-day mission time frames

Ninety-day mission time frames are long enough to achieve something significant yet short enough to force us to act now and not procrastinate. We plan first, then adapt as we encounter different circumstances. We could aim for focused Invitation Sundays in September, December, March and June. I really recommend Mission Action Planning as an excellent tool to help not only in a ninety-day time frame, but across all mission activities.[10]

Within a ninety-day mission time frame we can get into the habit of inviting guests home for dinner (see Romans 12:13). We can offer hospitality to one another (1 Peter 4:9). We don't forget to entertain strangers (Hebrews 13:2).

When you give a lunch or dinner, don't invite only your friends (Luke 14:12). Invite those you don't know well yet. This hospitality should be offered throughout the ninety days, with a focused Invitation Sunday at the end.

Ninety-day time frames help us to get into the Christian practice of radical hospitality. When people can't yet see the light of Christ, help them feel the heat of God's love!

The six secrets of becoming the best inviter in your church

1. Get serious about spending time with unchurched friends.

2. Identify your limiting factor and work on it, whether it is your confidence or your time management.

3. Look out all the time for potential friendships.

4. Visualize yourself bringing many of your friends and acquaintances to church.

5. Talk to yourself positively: "I am an inviter for Christ!"

6. Put the secrets into action!

The Sower triplet

You might find this helpful:

1. If every one of us aspired to be the best inviter in the congregation, we would see the fruit of God in both rejection and acceptance.

2. I'm going to be the best inviter. Will you join me?

3. I am going to ask each of you to be the best inviter with me.

Set high goals

Finally, I have discovered that my over-enthusiasm for God is not over-enthusiastic enough. To counteract discouragement and complacency, we need to move in the opposite direction. We need to be full of joy and confidence in God. I know this is generally not very Western, and I have been accused of being too enthusiastic at times. There is, of course, a quiet, deep, and sure faith which is apparent in peaceful certainty as well as more outward confidence. But introvert or extrovert, we need more confidence and certainty in our God.

Set your goals for God high. If you have a goal for God's work that is small, then the result will be small. One of the problems of the church today is that our goals are too low and we meet them. If we want to achieve great things for God, we must have much bigger goals. If we set higher goals, we will need to think in a different way. We need to rethink our goals for God and then multiply them by a factor of ten. How many more people will our churches serve and reach if we multiply our goals by ten?

Everything has to change when you are trying to reach a higher goal. It will change who you have to become, what your church has to become, and how many more people you will have to serve. We need to raise our standards and stretch our intentions for God.

Be aware that if your mind tells you, "I am sure about reaching this goal", then it is not high enough!

Are you contagiously enthusiastic about the work that you are doing? The enormous untapped capability of our church congregations and leaders gives me great hope for the future of the church. The difference between extraordinary church members and ordinary church members is that extraordinary church members take the first step, and as they take the first step, another step appears, and the enormous untapped potential that was there all along gradually materializes.

Extraordinary Christians choose the activity that will make the greatest contribution to the lives of those around them – the activity which best serves our Father's purposes. We are always free to choose. Extraordinary Christians just use their time better. Extraordinary Christians plant trees under whose branches they know they will never sit. They unlock the growth in their own lives and in the lives of those around them.

Questions to think about

- Can we imagine people actually spontaneously inviting on any and every ordinary Sunday, rather than having to wait for a special Sunday?

- One of the reasons churches stop inviting is because of disappointment. Did things always work out for Jesus? If not, give some examples.

- Must everything work first time for us today?

- Do we have to get our churches right before we invite?

- Which is more important, an act of worship or invitational mission? Should invitation be confined to only a couple of special Sundays? What does God tell us about this?

Appendix 1

The Twelve Steps Learning Tool

When you encourage invitation, it is always good to review how things went afterwards. Here is a learning tool that may be useful for a review:

- Step 1: Did the church leader manage to communicate, in a compelling way, the vision of doubling our congregation?

- Step 2: Did the church leader model invitation by inviting someone?

- Step 3: Did every member of the congregation get a personal invitation from the church leader or the leadership team to invite a friend?

- Step 4: Did we explain the spirituality of friendship?

- Step 5: Did we use the power of story?

- Step 6: Did we ask God who He might want us to invite?

- Step 7: Did we practise the question, "Would you like to

come to church with me?"

- Step 8: Did we pray as a church?

- Step 9: Did the congregation courageously make invitations?

- Step 10: Did we walk or drive to church with our guests?

- Step 11: Did we introduce our invited guests to our friends at church?

- Step 12: Did we invite them again the following week?

On scale of 1 to 10, with 1 being "poor" and 10 being "excellent", evaluate how things went.

Out of 120, how did you do?

If you scored 80 and above: You are igniting spontaneous invitation!

If you scored 40–80: God has given you the agenda for your congregation in the areas where you have a low score.

If you scored less than 40: Well done for trying invitation, but don't stop now! The learning tool above should help you to work on the areas to improve for next time.

Appendix 2

Back to Church Sunday – Perspectives from around the World

New Zealand – Archdeacon Tony Gerritsen

The concept of Back to Church Sunday is so elementary that it's surprising that it has not been thought of before; all credit to the B2CS team in the UK! It's simply about a friend inviting a friend to come and join them in worship. It sits at the heart of hospitality and really begs the question, why wouldn't Christians do this (because generally they don't)? So why? If this personal relationship with Jesus is so life-changing, if we give our lives to Him, if we are prepared to commit around three to four hours on a Sunday to the whole worship experience (preparation, travel, the service itself, post-worship socializing) when sports, cafés, and shopping all compete for our time, if it's that important to us, then why aren't we falling over ourselves to invite neighbours and friends to attend? Back to Church asks us to stop and ask ourselves, "Why not?"

Maybe some of it's about an innate shyness; maybe

some of it's about the three things we never talk about at dinner ("Religion is a private thing"); or is it simply that we're rather embarrassed about what our worship service offers on Sundays? Whatever the reason, it just doesn't mirror the gospel enthusiasm of the men and women in the Bible who got very excited about Jesus, and how their radically different way of living saw many being added to their number daily.

In New Zealand B2CS began well, with an average of nineteen people per congregation coming back to church when invited by a friend on the day set aside in both 2008 and 2009. The programme focused on a twenty-week preparation plan covering one issue a week: good coffee (instant just isn't so "in" any more); reflecting on the words of hymns (what invitee would understand "Jesus Lamb of God Messiah" without a wee bit of theological explanation?); toilets well labelled and brought up to scratch; can we try not to give them three books and two news-sheets? – to name but four issues. It was essentially a Warrant of Fitness check to make sure that we felt more confident about inviting people to something – church – that we were proud of.

B2CS is one of a variety of initiatives to draw people back to God… or to God for the first time. Fresh Expressions of Church, Pioneer Ministry, and various new monastic endeavours are other ways in which Christians are aiming to draw people to Jesus. The intentionality of all of these is to be encouraged and given personal and corporate prayer support.

Between the two World Wars Archbishop William

Temple reminded us that the church is the only society that exists for the benefit of its non-members. Jesus, a few centuries earlier, said, "Go, make disciples!" (Matthew 28:15ff). Back to Church Sunday is a rather easy way to do that. Others have got the show all set up; we just need to turn up with our friend(s) – and I have a feeling that heaven will smile.

Australia – Andrew W. Curnow

Today, across the world the church faces great challenges. In the First World it is decline and a loss of confidence. In the Third World it is a lack of resources. In both worlds the church needs to welcome all people in a positive and encouraging manner.

My experience is from the Anglican church in Australia, where we Anglicans represent about 25 per cent of the Christian community, but less than 5 per cent of Anglicans are regular churchgoers. Churchgoing in Australia has never really been strong compared with the United States, and the only time churches have been reasonably full was during the two World Wars, and especially after World War II. So very few Anglicans actually regularly attend church, but on the National Census large numbers still put down Anglican as their religious affiliation. For years I have tried various things to address this challenge. Then, in 2007, I began to hear about Back to Church Sunday and its emerging success in England. We have now just completed our third national Back to Church Sunday in the Anglican church of Australia and the signs are promising.

Let me tell you of a couple of concrete examples. In a small town called Kyneton, the local Anglican parish organized a small committee to prepare for Back to Church Sunday. The committee soon identified a significant list of names of people who had previously been involved with the local church or were known to them as occasional Anglicans. The committee undertook first to call everyone on the list and tell them about Back to Church Sunday. Then the invitations were delivered and followed up by another telephone call from one of the volunteers on the committee. Transport requirements were noted, along with any other special requests. On Back to Church Sunday, I was there to preach and welcome the invitees. The church was full, and the place was abuzz with excitement. It was a great service and I will always remember a conversation afterwards at morning tea. I talked with a woman who had lived in the town for some years and who, although a regular Anglican in her previous community, had never joined in Kyneton. I asked her how she decided to come today and reconnect. She very quickly gave me the answer: "The personal invitation" she said! Her answer was loud and clear.

From my long experience in ministry there is no substitute for a personal invitation. The phone, the internet, Facebook – all these can help, but in the end there is nothing better than someone in person saying, "Come and See".

Bob Jackson writing in his study book, *Everybody Welcome*, says: "Most churches think they are a friendly church because church members are friendly with each other.

We may not realize how unwelcoming we are to the outsider. But churches that do welcome and befriend the stranger are creating the sort of growing, flourishing community that Jesus wants his church to be".[1]

Fundamental to being a welcoming church is being an inviting church and that's where Back to Church Sunday is a golden opportunity.

Canada – Bishop Philip Poole

For three years the Diocese of Toronto has adopted "Back to Church Sunday" as a key part of our missional strategy to reach out to others in the name of Our Lord. Parishioners have been encouraged to invite their friends and neighbours to come to church with them on the last Sunday in September, to experience life in the Christian community.

As bishops we wanted to model for our members the act of inviting people to come to church. For the past three years, early in the morning on the Thursday before Back to Church Sunday, the five bishops of the diocese have donned cope and mitre, and stood outside the large commuter train stations in Toronto, personally handing invitations to the somewhat startled, bleary-eyed commuters. We did this primarily to encourage our parishioners to invite someone else to church, but the resulting publicity in the secular press has been very encouraging. As we discovered, inviting people to church takes way more courage than inviting someone to come to the theatre or a sporting event!

After three years the numerical results have been

impressive. We credit Back to Church Sunday with adding the equivalent of nearly six strong new parishes of 150 people. Six new parishes in three years in one diocese. Wow! It has added a certain confidence to some of our parishes and of course helped to change people's lives in the process. Over 5500 invitations were accepted and with an average retention rate of 15 per cent we can track about 825 new attendees.

More importantly, as we hoped, the notion of inviting people to church is beginning to seep into our collective diocesan DNA. One parish priest wrote, "We have a culture of inviting people to church throughout the year. And I think that Back to Church Sunday has had something to do with that". Another reports, "I just want to share with you that our parish had a great success with our Back to Church Sunday … we had over 50 newcomers and broke our record on a single Sunday attendance of 142. Even our next door parking lot was totally full. It was just so exciting to see new people." A large percentage of parishes reported some success resulting in an increase in attendance as a result of Back to Church Sunday.

But increased attendance is not the only or indeed true measure of success. Many parishes shared that their parishioners invited people to attend who did not take up the invitation. We have learned that success is in the inviting. It is between the Holy Spirit and the individual if he or she accepts. The block is in not inviting. We are seeking to make our church an inviting church.

After the first year those parishes which had numerical

Notes

Preface

1. Roy Hattersley, *The Life of John Wesley: A Brand from the Burning*, London: Little Brown, 2002.

2. Norman Doidge, *The Brain That Changes Itself*, New York: Penguin, 2007.

Chapter 1

1. Excerpts from Jim Rohn, *The Treasury of Quotes*, Jim Rohn International, 2002, www.jimrohn.com

2. Search 'Christianity Survey' in to the Open University website: http://www.open2.net/christianity/survey.html. Article used with permission.

Chapter 2

1. Donald Rumsfeld, *Known and Unknown: A Memoir*, New York: Sentinel, 2011.

2.This interpretation is borrowed from "The Parable of the Sower" on the audio CD *Building your Network Marketing Business*, Jim Rohn Audio.

3. Brian Tracy, *The 100 Absolutely Unbreakable Laws of Business Success*, San Francisco: Berrett-Koehler Publishers, 2002.

4. J. K. Galbraith, *Economics, Peace and Laughter: A Contemporary Guide*, Harmondsworth: Penguin, 1975, p. 50.

Chapter 3

1. For more on this subject see Bob Jackson and George Fisher, *Everybody Welcome*, London: Church House Publishing, 2009.

Chapter 4

1. The poem "Belief System" is believed to be by Charles Reade, but it is also variously attributed elsewhere.

2. John Dryden, quoted in Stephanie Goddard, *101 Ways to Love Your Job*, Naperville: Sourcebooks, 2008.

3. I was made aware of this phrase by the Revd Paul Vrolijk, the Anglican chaplain of Aquitaine in France.

4. www.thefreedictionary.com

Chapter 6

1. The Five Stages of Innovation, inspired by Alexander von Humboldt's "Three Stages Of Scientific Discovery", as referenced by Bill Bryson in his book, *A Short History Of Nearly Everything*.

Chapter 7

1. Chester and Betsy Kylstra, *Biblical Healing and Deliverance*, Grand Rapids: Chosen, 2005.

2. Terry Robson, *Failure is an Option: How setbacks breed success*, Sydney: Harper Collins, 2010.

3. Bishop N. T. Wright, *Jerusalem in the New Testament* (originally published in Peter Walker, *Jerusalem Past and Present in the Purposes of God*, Carlisle: Paternoster, 1994).

4. Norman Vincent Peale, *The Power of Positive Thinking*, New York: Prentice Hall, 1952.

5. Walter Bruggemann, *The Prophetic Imagination*, Minneapolis: Fortress Press, 1978.

6. Saint John of the Cross, "Dark Night of the Soul" (poem and treatise).

Chapter 8

1. Dwight Smith, "Why the church?", November 1998.

Chapter 9

1. The original quote was: "Be kind and merciful. Let no one ever come to you without coming away better and happier."

Conclusion

1. Dr Denis Waitley, *The Winners Edge: The Critical Attitude of Success*, Berkley Books, 1985.

2. Jim Rohn, *The Seasons of Life*, Discovery Publications, 1983.

3. Brian Tracy, *The 100 Absolutely Unbreakable Laws of Business Success*, San Francisco: Berrett-Koehler Publishers, 2002.

4. Brian Tracy, *The 100 Absolutely Unbreakable Laws of Business Success*.

5. G. K. Chesterton, *What's Wrong with the World?*, 1910.

6. Brian Tracy, *The 100 Absolutely Unbreakable Laws of Business Success*.

7. Brian Tracy, *The 100 Absolutely Unbreakable Laws of Business Success*.

8. Brian Tracy, *The 100 Absolutely Unbreakable Laws of Business Success*.

9. Brian Tracy, *The 100 Absolutely Unbreakable Laws of Business Success*.

10. Mark Ireland and Mike Chew, *How to do Mission Action Planning*, London: SPCK, 2009.

Appendix 3

1. Bob Jackson, *Everybody Welcome*, London: Church House Publishing, 2009, p. 5.